Secondary School Teaching and Educational Psychology

Secondary School Teaching and Educational Psychology

David Galloway and Anne Edwards

LONGMAN
London and New York

Longman Group UK Limited,
Longman House, Burnt Mill, Harlow,
Essex CM20 2JE, England
and Associated Companies throughout the world

Published in the United States of America
by Longman Publishing, New York

© Longman Group UK Limited 1992

First published 1992

ISBN 0-582-49724-8

British Library Cataloguing in Publication Data
A catalogue record for this book is
available from the British Library

Library of Congress Cataloging-in-Publication Data

Galloway, David, 1942–
   Secondary school teaching and educational psychology / David
Galloway and Anne Edwards.
      p. cm.--(Effective teacher series)
   Includes bibliographical references (p.) and index.
   ISBN 0-582-49724-8
   1. Educational psychology. 2. Problem children--Education
(Secondary)--Great Britain. 3. Special education--Great Britain.
I. Edwards, Anne, 1946– . II. Title. III. Series.
LB1051.G219 1992
370.15--dc20

                                            91–46054
                                            CIP

Set by 7E in 10/12 point Times
Printed in Malaysia by VVP

CONTENTS

EDITOR'S PREFACE

This new series was inspired by my book on the practice of teaching (*Effecting Teaching: a practical guide to improving your teaching*, Longman, 1982), written for trainee teachers wishing to improve their teaching skills as well as for in-service teachers, especially those engaged in the supervision of trainees. The books in this series have been written with the same readership in mind. However, busy classroom teachers will find that these books also serve their needs as changes in the nature and pattern of education make the in-service training of experienced teachers more essential than in the past.

The rationale behind the series is that professional courses for teachers require the coverage of a wide variety of subjects in a relatively short time. So the aim of the series is the production of 'easy to read', practical guides to provide the necessary subject background, supported by references to guide and encourage further reading, together with questions and/or exercises devised to assist application and evaluation.

As specialists in their selected fields, the authors have been chosen for their ability to relate their subjects to the needs of teachers and to stimulate discussion of contemporary issues in education.

The series aims to cover subjects ranging from the theory of education to the teaching of mathematics and from primary school teaching and educational psychology to effective teaching with information technology. It will look at aspects of education as diverse as education and cultural diversity and pupil welfare and counselling. Although some subjects such as the legal context of teaching and the teaching of history are specific to England and Wales, the majority of subjects such as assessment in education, the effective teaching of statistics and comparative education, are international in scope.

Elizabeth Perrott

AUTHORS' PREFACE

The 1980s saw far-reaching changes in the education system in Britain. While the introduction of the National Curriculum and local management of schools in the 1988 Education Reform Act had the greatest impact on school and classroom practice, the Education Acts of 1980, 1981 and 1986 each placed additional demands on teachers. One of the few things that successive Secretaries of State for Education and Science had in common with most teachers was a desire to raise educational standards. The legislative framework within which schools operate can facilitate or impede this goal, but the full effects of the 1988 Act, for better or worse, will probably not be evident until we are at the next millennium.

Nevertheless, it is quite clear that educational standards are not raised simply by ministerial, nor even parliamentary, diktat. They are raised by teachers who have a clear understanding (a) of the varying influences on children's development both in school and outside it and (b) of the processes that help children develop into effective, active learners, increasingly willing to undertake intellectually challenging tasks and increasingly able to take responsibility for much of their own learning. The rationale for this book is that educational psychology makes an important contribution in each respect. In other words, we aim to show how the psychology of education extends our understanding of teachers' day-to-day work in the classroom as well as of children with particular problems.

In writing the book we took a broad view of what constitutes educational psychology. Thus, we refer to research from developmental, social and clinical psychology where this has obvious implications for the world of the school. For the same reason we make no apology for giving prominence to work on classroom interaction that falls into the grey area between the psychology and the sociology of education.

Our overriding consideration, though, was that the book should address the immediate concerns of secondary school teachers. It should stand or fall by the extent to which it recognises their concerns and helps teachers to make sense of their work with children. Educational psychology no longer enjoys its former prominent place in initial teacher training. This is partly the result of changes in teacher training imposed by the government. It is also the result of widespread and entirely legitimate dissatisfaction with much of what has in the past been taught in the name of educational psychology. In particular, we aimed to avoid three common criticisms:

1. Many books, and the courses on which they were used, were over-theoretical, with insufficient links between theory and classroom practice. Consequently, they did little to extend teachers' understanding of their own work in the classroom.
2. Few books, if any, have made any serious attempt to identify the common ground between educational psychology and other disciplines, such as the sociology and philosophy of education.
3. There was often an over-emphasis on the psychology of the individual child, with a correspondingly inadequate attention to children's learning in the social context of the classroom.

If our book was to be useful, we believed it would have to avoid a 'Cook's Tour' approach to educational psychology, with its comprehensive but necessarily superficial itinerary through all the main centres of influence. A consequence of this decision was that it demanded an inevitably idiosyncratic selection of the work of psychologists which seemed to us of greatest importance for teachers. In particular, four themes recur throughout the book:

1. The varied and interacting influences of home, the extended family, the school and the classroom (among others) on children's development.
2. The interactive nature of teaching, and the ways in which teachers and children affect each other's behaviour.
3. The importance, both for teachers and for children, of 'metacognitive' skills, i.e. the ability to reflect on the nature of a task, to recognise the demands it makes and to identify appropriate ways of overcoming them.
4. The links between educational psychology and other disciplines.

The final point deserves further explanation. The interests of psychologists do not arise purely from the disinterested pursuit of knowledge. They are grounded in philosophical views of the aims of education and the nature of childhood. Further, many of the concerns of educational psychologists are shared by sociologists and by philosophers. We aim to make these links explicit.

Scope of the book

Educational psychology contains two related but oddly independent traditions. First, the principal concern of educational psychologists employed by LEAs is to provide guidance and advice about the education of children with special educational needs. Their principal concern is thus with children who, for some reason, have been identified as problems. Secondly, academic psychologists have been more concerned, at least recently, with classroom interaction and with the processes involved in effective teaching and learning. Their starting point is the 'normal' classroom. This second tradition is sometimes known as the psychology of education, to distinguish its principal focus from that of educational psychologists. We do not find this distinction helpful. We regard the two traditions as complementary and draw on both in the course of the book.

After an introductory chapter, Chapter 2 examines contextual influences on teachers' understanding of children and on children's own development. This leads into Chapter 3, which reviews recent thinking about provision for children with special educational needs, especially learning and behavioural difficulties. Because the needs of these children cannot be seen in isolation from those of all other children in the class, Chapter 4 considers recent work on classroom interaction. Chapter 5 analyses the ways in which teachers and pupils can make sense of their experience in school and Chapter 6 approaches the vexed issue of classroom management from the position that effective management of behaviour is inextricably linked to management of learning through the curriculum. Because teachers and parents regard schools as having responsibilities which extend beyond the National Curriculum, Chapter 7 focuses on personal and social development. Chapter 8 draws together the themes of assessment and evaluation that have been introduced in previous chapters. The final chapter provides an overview and discusses a model for professional development.

Why separate books on primary school teaching and secondary school teaching?

This book has the same format, and the same chapter headings, as our earlier book *Primary School Teaching and Educational Psychology*. We originally hoped they would be published simultaneously, but this proved impossible. In theory we could have written a single book incorporating examples relevant to primary and secondary schools, with separate sections for discussion of issues applying specifically to each sector. In practice we felt strongly that this would have limited the usefulness of the book, both for students and practising teachers, and for university or college tutors. Separate volumes seemed important for two reasons.

First, any book for commencing teachers should, as we said earlier, address their *immediate* concerns. Second, we believe that the principal contribution of educational psychology to the thinking and practice of commencing teachers lies in helping them to evaluate and make sense of their *current* classroom experience. For both reasons we felt that a single volume would dilute the message. On the other hand, we recognised that the Professional Studies component of many BEd and PGCE programmes contains a course of lectures attended jointly by secondary and primary students. Hence, the similar format of each volume acknowledges the common ground, while providing opportunities for follow-up in small groups of teachers specialising in each sector.

Using the book

Each chapter is followed by suggestions for further reading and seminar activities. The book is designed for use by practising secondary school teachers and by students on BEd and PGCE courses. It is intended to contribute to teachers' and students' professional awareness. Ideally, professional studies are integrated into the individual's own experience in the classroom. The seminar suggestions indicate some of the ways this can be achieved. Our broader aims are (a) to encourage people to review and evaluate their own experience as teachers and as learners, and (b) to arouse an interest in ways that educational psychology and other disciplines contribute to an understanding of effective teaching and learning. The book could be evaluated by the quality of discussion it provokes. As Margaret Sutherland said in her preface to *The Theory of Education*, we are sorry we shall be unable to take part in the discussion.

David Galloway and Anne Edwards
January 1992

NOTE ON AUTHORSHIP

Planning and writing this book was a cooperative venture. Inevitably, though, there was some division of responsibilities. Each chapter went through at least two drafts as we took account of each other's criticisms. For the record, Chapters 1–3, 7 and 9 were written mainly by David Galloway, and Chapters 4–6 and 8 mainly by Anne Edwards.

DEDICATION

This book is dedicated to our long-suffering families.

ACKNOWLEDGEMENTS

We are grateful to the numerous students and teachers who have criticised, modified and helped to develop our thinking. Parts of Chapters 2 and 7 are reproduced from David Galloway's book *Pupil Welfare and Counselling* (Longman, 1990).

The Publishers are grateful to the following for permission to reproduce copyright material:

Harper Collins for Table 1.1 adapted from *Motivation and Personality*, 2nd edition, by Abraham H. Maslow. Copyright 1970 Abraham H. Maslow; The Journal of Philosophy, Columbia University, New York and the author Lawrence Kohlberg, for Table 7.1 – Definition of Moral Stages from *The Claim to Moral Adequacy of a Highest Stage of Moral Judgment*, Journal of Philosophy, **LXX**, **18**, (October 25, 1973): 631–2 (version).

LIST OF FIGURES AND TABLES

DISCLAIMERS

The views expressed in this book are the authors' own and should not be taken to reflect those of their employers, nor of individuals or institutions who cooperated with any of the inquiries referred to in the book. When presenting case histories and when quoting teachers or pupils verbatim we have changed names, abbreviations of names, nicknames and other identifying characteristics.

CHAPTER 1

Getting started: understanding children's needs

Introduction

It is difficult to talk for long about teaching, educational psychology or any other work with children and young people without thinking about their personal, social and educational needs. Indeed, professionals working with children and teenagers exist to meet their presumed needs. Parents, too, often agonise over what would be best for one or more of their children. Yet there is no more agreement about the nature of the needs of secondary school pupils than about the needs of any other age-group. Different people emphasise the importance of different needs, depending not on any absolute psychological or educational truths but on their own background and priorities.[1] Thus one of Her Majesty's Inspectors of schools (HMI) might talk about the need for a 'broad and balanced' curriculum, a child psychiatrist about the need for teachers to provide their more vulnerable pupils with a warm, supportive relationship, and a politician, with an eye on the law and order vote, about the need for discipline.

This book is about the applications of psychology, and in particular educational psychology in secondary schools. It assumes that ideas developed by educational psychologists have some value in helping teachers to understand their pupils' needs. Yet teachers could reasonably claim to be bewildered by the range of needs they are expected to meet. They could also claim that the concept of need is itself hopelessly confused. For example, when adults say that teenagers *need* to belong to a youth club or similar group, do they mean that parents *ought* to make a special effort to encourage this, that teenagers have a *right* to group membership, that it is a universal psychological *requirement*, or all three? In this chapter we examine what we mean when talking about the needs of secondary school pupils. We shall then look at two ways of understanding adolescents' needs, and finally consider their usefulness for teachers in secondary schools.

What do we mean when talking about children's needs?

Following the 1988 Education Reform Act, the National Curriculum was introduced into schools in Britain. This summarises what the

Department of Education and Science (DES) thinks pupils need to, or should, learn in the years of compulsory education. The National Curriculum represents one view of children's needs. Another 'official' view is represented in the Teachers Conditions of Service document (DES,1988a) which requires teachers to have regard to pupils' 'general progress and well-being'. Clearly, this implies that teachers' responsibilities for their pupils extend beyond the curriculum to include their welfare or pastoral needs. Professional opposition to the National Curriculum was both strong and united (Haviland, 1988). Teachers did not think a National Curriculum would help them meet their pupils' educational needs more effectively.[2]

This is all pretty remote, though, from the concerns of parents as their children start at secondary school. By definition, this is a time of transition. It would be odd if some parents did not remember their secondary schooling with little satisfaction or pleasure. Inevitably, such memories affect the family's preparations for the start of the new term. Similarly, some parents see transition to secondary school as the start of a new and potentially difficult stage in their relationship with their child. Yet initially most parents probably define their children's needs in terms such as (a) 'settling in' well; (b) making friends; (c) finding interesting things in the school's programme of extra-curricular activities; (d) making 'good' progress in their work. The last of these is by no means the least. Performance in the public examinations in year 11, the final year of compulsory schooling, will open the door to a wide range of jobs, or close it. Being placed in the top stream or band, or in a high set will affect their child's chances.[3] For many children, starting a new school is a time of increasing academic pressure.

Yet even this is pretty remote from the immediate needs both of children and of their teachers as they start secondary school. What pupils expect will be influenced by what they have heard from friends, neighbours or older brothers and sisters. At least for boys, part of the national folklore of primary–secondary transition seems to be that awful things will happen at some stage in the first two terms. Having your head put down the toilet is perhaps the most common piece of folklore. The evidence that these initiation rites still persist is thankfully scarce – there are rumours that even public schools are becoming humane – though in the 1980s there were schools in which staff regarded the 'pinning' of first-year boys as a persistent but insoluble problem. This ritual involved older boys holding down newcomers, when no teachers were around, and sticking pins into their buttocks.

Not surprisingly, transfer to secondary school is a time of anxiety. How much anxiety is felt depends partly on the child, partly on their parents' attitudes and partly on preparation for transfer in the last term or two at primary school. There is evidence from the ORACLE study that primary children feel cynical about 'set piece' visits from secondary school staff. They are equally cynical about formal tours of the secondary school. On the other hand, the opportunity to spend a day attending lessons in the secondary school before they actually transfer does seem to be reassuring (Galton and Willcocks, 1983). Indeed, in the first few days, reassurance and finding their way around may be children's most pressing needs.

Above all, they will consciously be adapting to a new and complex set of expectations: the expectations of teachers, of other children in their year group and of older pupils. Sometimes these expectations conflict. Teachers expect you to wear the school uniform in the officially approved way, but second-year pupils laugh at you for the tidy way you tie your tie. To avoid being laughed at, you learn not to do up the top button of your shirt and to pull the tie into a tightly tangled knot, preferably hanging at half mast.

Teachers, too, are adapting to a new and complex set of expectations. The new pupils are likely to come from several different primary schools. In many schools there will be a mixed ability group, ranging from the exceptionally able to children with a range of learning difficulties. The teacher has to find out what each child can do, who can be relied on to take messages, who 'needs watching' and so on. They identify children's needs informally, through discussion with each other and by developing their own categorisation systems. These are no different in nature from the informal categorisations used in any social relationships. In the same way, people classify their neighbours by their hobby, by occupation, by political inclination and by the behaviour of their children ('the ones with the rowdy teenagers') or by whether they are interesting to talk to.

Unfortunately, this informal categorising is often unreliable and can lead teachers to underestimate children's ability, particularly in their first year at secondary school. There is evidence that many children make little progress in their first year, often spending their time going over ground they covered in their primary school (Delamont and Galton, 1986). As newcomers in their new school they lack the confidence to protest and their acquiescence in, for them, undemanding tasks may be taken as evidence that they are working to an appropriate level.

Nor should we forget the systematic if informal assessments that take place in every classroom at the start of the year. From the outset, teachers are formulating and testing theories about the class as a whole and about individuals in the class. They may not do this consciously, but teaching cannot take place without assessment, and assessment takes place at several different levels (see Chapter 8). At the most basic level teachers are noting behaviour that helps or hinders the smooth running of the class, and identifying possible ways to encourage or discourage it. At the same time, children are formulating and testing theories about each of their teachers: will Mr Jones 'flip' if we carry on talking when he told us to be quiet in the same way that Miss Owen did? What happens if we only do one page of homework instead of the two pages we were told to do?

Quickly, and often without conscious effort, children adapt their behaviour in the the light of their experience. Following a class from lesson to lesson reveals how effectively they 'learn' to behave in different ways with different teachers (see Rabinowitz, 1981). More important, what they learn from their teachers' reactions starts to influence what they feel about the school. For some, school becomes a place where they feel valued, where they know that their efforts will be recognised and where they do interesting things in the classroom and in extra-curricular activities. For others school becomes a place where they are made to feel stupid, both by teachers and by other pupils. For teachers the position is more complex. Their sense of security will be affected by a variety of factors, varying from the nature of their contract, the quality of support from the head, and the amount of resources available. It is also affected by their own success in classroom organisation and management. This is partly a question of organising the available resources in a way that arouses the children's interest and partly of organising the children themselves so that they benefit from the learning experiences provided. Failure on either count will be evident in the children's behaviour, as they feel increasingly unsettled, restless and unsure of themselves. Teachers depend for their job satisfaction and their self-esteem on seeing children making progress within the classroom environment they have created. It follows that there is a close relationship between teachers' definition of their pupils' needs and the needs of teachers themselves.

Needs, wants and rights

As well as the informal assessment involved in any social interaction, teachers also use more formal procedures to define children's needs. While the introduction of the National Curriculum may replace some of the standardised reading and maths tests whose sales keep research foundations and publishers solvent, some LEAs are introducing mass testing in order to adjust the funding provided to each school in the light of the proportion of pupils who have special educational needs. Clearly, intelligence and educational attainment tests are assessment techniques as well as aids to identifying and understanding children's needs. The point is that logically we cannot talk about children's needs not being met without having first made an assessment that they lack something important to their development. Similarly, in claiming that we are meeting a child's needs we claim that we are providing the things we consider important to his or her development.

The important issue here is that the things a teacher considers most important to a child's or teenager's development may not coincide with what the young person's parent considers most important. Different people give priority to different needs. This is partly a matter of professional affiliation. Teachers can no longer work in isolation, if indeed this was ever the case. They are accountable to their head teacher, and through the head to the school's governors and to their employers, all of whom have more or less clear expectations as to what pupils should be achieving at school. Some of these expectations are now enshrined in a National Curriculum. Inevitably they affect how teachers define pupils' needs. Other professionals, such as social workers or doctors, have different responsibilities and are accountable to other bodies. Consequently they define children's needs in different terms. Thus, a social worker might emphasise the importance of a secure family life, while a social psychologist might be concerned foremost with the individual's developing awareness of being part of a social community.

In each case the assessment of what children need is based on what the person concerned 'wants' for the child. It also implies that the person thinks that children have a right to have their needs met. Hence in talking about pupils' needs we are making a value judgement about what *we* think should be provided for them. Unfortunately there are two complicating factors here:

1. There is no agreement within the teaching profession, nor between teachers, other professionals or the government, on what constitutes children's and young people's rights. In passing the 1988 Education Reform Act the government implicitly stated that parents have a right to know what their children will be taught. The introduction of the National Curriculum reflected the government's assessment that schools were providing an inadequate education for an unacceptably high percentage of pupils. In claiming that educational provision was inadequate, the government was making a value judgement. Virtually all teacher associations disputed this value judgement and consequently saw no need for a National Curriculum. Teachers, parents or government committees may claim a 'scientific' basis for their concerns about children's needs, as in the Warnock Committee's claim that 20 per cent of pupils may be expected to require some form of special educational provision at some stage in their school career (DES, 1978a;, see Chapter 3). Ultimately, though, these claims come down to a value judgement on the part of the individuals or groups concerned. This is no criticism. Teaching is not value free and never can be. Moreover, as public employees, teachers are accountable to parents, governors and employers, and consequently cannot have complete autonomy in defining their pupils' needs.

2. The second problem is more complex. Teaching is a social
    activity, and teachers are accountable for the behaviour and
    progress of the class as a whole. In saying that a boy needs to
    learn to sit down, or that a girl needs to learn not to shout out,
    teachers are likely to be making a statement as much about their
    own need for control as about the child's need to learn an
    important social skill. This problem becomes even more acute in
    the case of children whose behaviour or educational progress
    gives cause for exceptional concern. The problem may lie in the
    resources available in the classroom, in the methods the teacher is
    using, or in the overall management and organisation of the
    classroom. The temptation, though, will be to define the problem
    in terms of the needs of an individual child or group of children.
    In other words needs are individualised: the pupil is said to have
    special needs as a way of avoiding recognition of the professional
    needs of the teacher. There are two implications. First, children's
    needs have to be seen in the context of the classroom and of the
    school. Secondly, if pupils are thought to have special needs, or
    even ordinary needs that are not adequately being met, this may
    have implications for the resources available to teachers and/or for
    their teaching methods.

Can we talk about 'psychological' needs?

We believe that educational psychology can help teachers to
understand their own experience in school and also their pupils', even
though changes in teacher training have unseated it from the central
position it once held (DES, 1989a).[4] This is quite different, however,
from claiming that it is possible to identify psychological needs as
opposed to personal, social or educational ones. A conventional
definition of psychology is the study of behaviour. We cannot talk
about personal, social or educational needs without implying that we
think children or people in their environment should behave in certain
ways. Even if we define psychology as the study of the mind, it is
logically impossible to think of psychological needs that do not imply
some form of behaviour. The behaviour may not be directly observable
– for example, thinking or reflection – but it is still behaviour.

Psychologists live and work in a social world as well as observing
it. Unfortunately, they sometimes make the mistake of trying to
identify children's needs in isolation, away from the context in which
they are living, working and playing. It does not follow, however, that
needs identified in the course of an educational psychologist's
one-to-one interview with a child can usefully be described as
psychological needs. The reason is simply that any identified needs
will have implications for the child's future behaviour and, almost

certainly, for that of teachers or parents. It follows that the needs identified by psychologists, like those identified by teachers, imply an interaction between children and the people in their environment.

Two ways of thinking about children's needs

A hierarchy of needs?

Maslow (1970) argued that people have a hierarchy of needs from the basic needs for food and drink to 'self-actualisation' or the sense of self-fulfilment that comes from achieving one's full potential. This hierarchy is summarised in Table 1.1. Maslow argued that people are only motivated to achieve higher level needs when lower level needs have not been met. In fact this is not always the case.

Table 1.1 **Summary of Maslow's hierarchy of needs**

Highest level:	'Self-actualisation'; the sense of self-fulfilment that comes from achieving one's full potential
	Aesthetic appreciation
	Intellectiual challenge and achievement
	Self-esteem: the need for approval and recognition
	Sense of belonging/membership of family, class, peer group
	Safety: the need to feel physically and psychologically secure
Lowest level:	Survival: basic needs for food, drink, etc.

Adapted from Maslow (1970)

Neither children nor adults always progress up the hierarchy in an orderly way. For example, the 12 year-old who joins his friends in a shop-lifting expedition or the 14 year-old who orders drinks in a pub because she thinks it is sophisticated, may be placing his or her need for approval and recognition from other young people before the need to feel 'physically and psychologically secure'. Nevertheless, two examples will illustrate how failure to meet lower-order needs on Maslow's hierarchy may affect pupils' progress, resulting in frustration for pupil and teacher alike. In both cases no amount of curriculum development or attention to teaching methods would have made much difference.

1. Jenny was a rather adenoidal girl in her second year at secondary school. Her primary school had said she missed a lot of time because of colds and minor infections. In the secondary school no teacher regarded her as a problem but the more observant described her as being 'in a world of her own'. She had a reputation for not listening to instructions, preferring to sit quietly where she wouldn't be noticed. She was far from being a high

flyer educationally, but most teachers said 'we've got a lot worse than Jenny!'. When she was 12 her mother took her to the doctor because she was unusually 'chesty'. The doctor confirmed that she had an infection, but also diagnosed catarrhal deafness, often known as 'glue ear', associated with colds, minor infections and hay fever. There were times when she had no hearing loss. Yet her tendency to 'switch off' rather than concentrate in order to hear what the teacher said, continued even when she was physically fit. Since she started school her education had been affected by her hearing loss. By the time it was diagnosed, secondary problems of loss of motivation had developed.

2. Some of the lower school classes in an urban comprehensive were based in portable classrooms in the school playground and these classes had a long-standing reputation for being hard to teach. When they moved and left the portable classrooms teachers noticed after a few weeks that they had become much easier to teach. Three years earlier a teacher had complained about the noise and flicker from the ancient strip-lights in the portable classrooms; the head had forwarded the complaint to County Hall but nothing had been done and the head had not persisted.

Maslow's hierarchy has limited usefulness as a psychological theory: people do not always behave in the ways it predicts. Nevertheless, it does illustrate the complex interrelationships involved in teaching. As both vignettes show, effective teaching cannot take place without attention to aspects of pupil welfare. Indeed, the interrelationship between teaching and welfare becomes even more evident when we consider the fourth need on Maslow's hierarchy, self-esteem.

Teachers can infer low esteem from children's reluctance to attempt something they may find difficult, from observing them to be fearful in new situations, from disparaging remarks they make about their own work, or from their general relationships with other pupils. Superficially the explanation may appear obvious, for example that the child has a minor physical disability, is 'slower' than other children educationally, or is constantly being compared with a more successful older brother or sister at home. Thus, how pupils with asthma or some other physical impairment see themselves may depend largely on how far their school has developed an ethos of pastoral care in which all teachers, not just pastoral care specialists, seek to create a climate which accepts and respects individual differences.

At the end of each year, or perhaps at the end of each term, teachers make 'adjustments' to the ability bands, or the sets in particular subjects. These adjustments result in some children being moved up, and others down. In some secondary schools parents are routinely consulted about such moves. In others parents hear about them from their children. Sometimes the first intimation comes from reading their children's annual report; children often feel there is no point in going out of their way to report bad news. Thus, ability is equated with status. Teachers often say that their less able groups have motivation problems. It may be the feeling that they have been labelled 'slow' rather than the low attainment as such which negatively affects their motivation.

Secondary teachers have been heard talking critically about pupils' difficult home circumstances, and attributing the pupils' lack of progress or difficult behaviour to these. Undoubtedly the home circumstances often *are* difficult. Nevertheless, schools vary widely in their success in establishing effective communication with their pupils' parents. A survey of Welsh secondary schools by Woods (1984) revealed huge differences between schools. A particularly striking point to emerge from this survey was that one of the most successful schools had a predominantly working-class pupil intake, thereby refuting the stereotype of parental disinterest.

Maslow's hierarchy of needs implicitly emphasises the importance of adults recognising and meeting children's needs. Obviously, teachers have to make assessments about their pupils' needs, but this should not obscure the fact that teaching is an interactive process to which children also contribute. The facts that the teacher is responsible for the classroom's stability, and that the child has to learn to work and play with other children, suggest another way of looking at children's needs.

Schooling as a process of adaptation

Meeting the needs of children is not simply a case of predicting or responding to the demands of pupils. The reality is far more complex. First, one purpose of schooling is to create citizens, skilled members of society. To that extent the needs of children may be defined by external forces rather than by schools. Teachers are themselves, therefore, severely constrained in the ways they are able to define, recognise and react to needs.

The perception of the child's need as either appropriate or inappropriate may well depend upon the 'climate' of the school. Galloway and Goodwin (1987) describe school climate as a network of relationships between pupils and teachers 'that determines what they expect of each other'. Climates vary and hence recognition of, and responses to, needs differ. The importance of climate to the development of a child as pupil and as citizen is highlighted by a perspective on child development provided by Shotter (1984). Borrowing a metaphor from ecology, he describes childhood itself as a 'niche' provided by society in which the child is allowed to develop.

Adolescence can, of course, be seen in the same way. Inherent in the concept of an ecological niche is the assumption that it provides a necessarily limited range of experiences. These enable the individual to develop into adulthood in a way that is appropriate to a particular society or social grouping. The child or adolescent may act on the niche to modify it, and hence its expectations or developmental opportunities. The most obvious example of this comes from the way in which adolescents assert their individuality through their dress and their behaviour. The popular belief in adolescent rebellion has been overstated; most adolescents do not reject their parents' values.[5] Nevertheless, it is not hard to see how they seek to create additional, or at least different opportunities thus modifying the niche in which they find themselves.

However, when Shotter's framework is applied to schooling it could be argued that there are considerable external pressures on the niche itself which inhibit any flexibility it might wish to have in responding to all the needs of pupils. Schools as niches that turn children into pupils are both constraining and constrained. They are constraining in the sense that they place obvious limits on what children can do. They are constrained in the sense that they have to operate within a legal framework and within the broad expectations of the school's governors and of the pupils' parents. In the primary years children are turned into pupils. In the secondary years schools are one of the agents through which society produces its future workers and parents. As Willes (1981, p. 61) has noted in another context, children may conform willingly and even actively in the school's activities. Nevertheless, 'to be a fully participating pupil is not necessarily to be an independent and well motivated learner'.

To this the response of teachers can only be that the converse, equally, is not necessarily the case. Two of the themes explored in this volume relate to ways in which children may become increasingly in control of their own learning processes and the importance of a sense of effectiveness and motivation to the success of that endeavour. That this is to be achieved within the constraints operating in schools as providers of 'schooling' means that any examination of children in schools needs to take the context of their behaviours or experiences into full consideration.

Relevance for secondary school teachers

We have outlined two ways of thinking about children's needs in the classroom. How, in their different ways, do Maslow and Shotter help teachers to recognise the varying influences on children's experience in the classrooom, and indeed on their own? One answer is suggested from research on effective teaching. This suggests that children can acquire the skill of 'metacognition', or the ability to monitor the demands of a task and to take appropriate action to solve problems they encounter. In other words, children have learned to recognise when they find a task difficult and to work out why. They may seek help from the teacher or they may have learned to find a solution for themselves. In either case they are starting to become autonomous, since they are not solely dependent on the teacher for approval or guidance. By thinking about, or reflecting on, what they are doing, they are learning how to learn. Two examples illustrate this process.

1.   Jason and Ahmed are working independently in a craft and design project. Their aim is to make a loud buzzer which sounds when their front door is opened, as a way of deterring intruders. At the design stage both boys have been given guidance on possible ways to achieve this goal, ranging from pressure pads under the doormat to use of an invisible beam. Jason works mainly by trial and error. He has ideas, but soon sees problems in each of them; then, instead of analysing how the problem arose, he rejects the idea itself as unsound. He soon gets frustrated and makes no useful progress. Ahmed, too, has ideas. He, too, sees problems, but instead of rejecting the idea he talks to himself about why they arose. He asks himself what made him think the idea could work, and how could he find a way round the problem he has identified. He also tries to anticipate problems: 'What happens if someone comes to the door and then goes away? That will leave the buzzer on and run down the battery.' The two boys do equally well on tasks requiring recall of factual material, but in the design task Ahmed is much more successful.

2.   A fourth-year GCSE class is working on a project on the history of buildings in the area. Jenny elects to study the history of the local church. Having failed to find anything in the school library, she is told the name of the author of a history of the church, published twenty years ago. This is missing from the school library. She is told where in the town library she will be able to see another copy. Having read this, she returns to her teacher for further help and is told about the history of churches in the diocese. Next she is told to look in the archives of the local newspaper. At each step she asks for advice and her teacher gives it. In the next class Sharon's project is on the materials used to build the church. With the other pupils, she makes a list of possible sources of information. Her teacher seldom provides explicit information, but instead aims to guide her learning: 'You haven't said much about the roof timbers; what could you want to find out about them?' Sharon does not immediately find much information, but when she draws a blank she explores ways to get round the problem. Before long she has discovered that different

timbers were used in different parts of the roof, the reasons (economy), and the consequences (the ash was attacked by woodworm but the pitch pine and the oak were still sound).

Metacognitive skills do not just develop. They are learned from observation of other children, from the way the teachers organise children's learning and from the nature of feedback they give children. Teaching is not only about the transmission of facts and never has been. It is also concerned with teaching children how to learn. An essential element in this is the ability to monitor what they are doing and to adapt their strategies in the light of this.

Perhaps the most important function of theory in education is to help teachers acquire the metacognitive skills they wish to develop in their pupils. Theories, then, are useful if they help teachers to reflect on their own practice, and to evaluate it. Monitoring one's own teaching cannot be divorced from monitoring the children's progress. It implies that the climate and organisation of the classroom and everything else in the nebulous but important concept of teaching quality, will affect their development.

A theory should do more, however, than help teachers to reflect on and to evaluate their own practice. It should also give them the ability, or power, to modify or develop their classroom practice. In other words, theories are useful if teachers can use them to generate and test theories of their own. Teaching can be seen as a constant process of generating and testing ideas, or theories, about children's knowledge, understanding, skills, attitudes and behaviour. Understandably, teachers repeat strategies that have proved successful in the past. Often these have been discovered by a lengthy process of trial and error, which is a notoriously inefficient way of learning. Also, some teachers have blind spots about important aspects of their pupils' development. The work of psychologists, as of educational sociologists, historians and philosophers can be seen as an aid to monitoring and evaluating their own experience and thereby exploring ways of improving it.[6]

Conclusions

How a person defines children's needs will depend as much on that person's background and priorities as on the children themselves. Moreover, it makes no sense to talk about children's needs in isolation from the context in which they are living, working and playing. In this chapter we have looked at two ways of thinking about the needs of secondary school pupils. Maslow's hierarchy of needs is well known but has limited value as a psychological theory. Shotter's notion of schooling as an ecological niche also has limitations as a theory – it is hard to disprove, but does indicate how pupils and teachers may affect each other's environment. Our assumption throughout the chapter has been that teaching is a social activity. Hence we must now turn to other ways of thinking about the complex interactions that take place in all classrooms.

Notes and further reading

1.   For a discussion of the interrelationships in children's educational, personal and social development see Galloway (1990a).
2.   Teachers work within a legislative framework. Their perceptions of the impact of recent legislation are also likely to affect their underlying sense of security. For a useful discussion of the 1988 Education Reform Act, see McClure (1989). A more sharply critical view is given by Simon (1989).
3.   In a streamed school, each class in a year-group is graded according to presumed ability; children are then taught *all* subjects in the same class. This bizarre practice assumes that children are equally competent in all areas of the curriculum – for example, that an outstanding mathematician is also outstanding at English, and vice versa. It is now mercifully rare. Banding involves grouping children into two or occasionally three ability groups, but within each band all classes in a year-group are of mixed ability. Setting is effectively streaming by subject. A pupil could be in a high set in one subject and a low set in another. Many schools have mixed ability classes for some subjects, and setting for others. In addition, banding and setting are often combined.
4.   The Council for Accreditation of Teacher Education (CATE) has produced a set of criteria which all initial teacher training courses are required to satisfy (see DES, 1989a). For a discussion of the controversies surrounding psychology's contribution to education, see Claxton *et al.* (1985).
5.   See Coleman and Hendry (1990).
6.   An excellent introduction to the theory of education is provided in Sutherland (1988).

For two more general books relating theoretical perspectives to classroom practice, see Cohen and Manion (1981) and Woolfolk and Nicolich (1980).

Seminar suggestions

1.   Examine the prospectus for each school in which members of the group have most recently worked. Do they differ in the way they talk about children's needs?
2.   From the perspective of militant members of each of the two main political parties, write entries on the psychological needs of children for a school prospectus. Consider the different priorities that emerge from this exercise, and discuss how far Maslow's hierarchy of needs has a 'political' or ideological basis.

3.   Drawing on Shotter's concept of childhood as an ecological 'niche', write a short (up to one page) account of one pupil's adaptation to a new school/class. Compare different accounts, and consider: (a) how the pupil was helped/encouraged to adapt to the requirements of the classroom; (b) whether the pupil succeeded in modifying the classroom in any way.

CHAPTER 2

Similarities and differences

Introduction

Priorities and values

Educational psychology in Britain has been preoccupied with individual differences since Cyril Burt became the then London County Council's first educational psychologist in 1913. How we think about individual differences depends on what we believe an education service should be providing, how we view a state's responsibility to its citizens and vice versa. In other words it depends on our priorities and values.

Let us start by considering a conventional argument. If teachers claim to be meeting the needs of individual pupils they must necessarily have an interest in individual differences, unless they believe, naively, that all pupils are the same. If educational psychologists aim to help teachers meet their pupils' needs, they too must have an interest in individual differences. This argument appears so eminently reasonable as hardly to be worth stating. In fact, it *is* eminently reasonable if we accept the premise on which it is based, namely that teachers are trying to meet the needs of all their pupils. After all, if pupils are not all the same, as they manifestly are not, it would surely be grossly unfair to teach them all in exactly the same way. An awareness of individual differences will merely help teachers to see how to adapt the curriculum to the needs of the child.

Unfortunately, the premise is contentious. As we shall argue throughout this book, teachers are not free agents. They are accountable to their colleagues, the school governors, their pupils' parents and to the pupils themselves. Moreover, neither teacher nor pupils start the school year with a *tabula rasa*; they have all come to internalise certain beliefs, values and prejudices that will influence how they think about individual differences and how they behave towards each other. These constitute the hidden agenda, or unstated reasons, for an interest in individual differences. We consider four arguments below:

1. Categorising pupils by ability, behaviour or gender is an organisational convenience. Boys and girls can be seated on

separate sides of the hall in assembly, special provision can be made for pupils with learning difficulties and a pastoral care network can provide support for, and supervision of, the troublesome minority of pupils who need a close eye to be kept on them.

2. Categorising pupils legitimises the teacher's own preconceptions about the groups concerned: 'Boys get out of hand if you don't crack down at the start of the year'; 'Girls can be so spiteful to each other'; 'We mustn't expect too much as we know all about the home background'; 'He can't read because he's dyslexic'; 'Black children are often rowdy'. The expected ability and behaviour of boys/girls, ethnic minority pupils, pupils with professional parents or pupils with special needs can form part of any teacher's or psychologist's personal value system. By organising a class around recognition of such differences we are merely creating the conditions which reinforce this value system, or to put it another way, which strengthen our prejudices and thereby remove any need to confront and question them.

3. Categorising pupils enables us to remove them from the classroom by shunting them into a low-status siding which is then legitimised as intending to meet their special needs (see Chapter 3). This can happen when teachers allocated to special needs withdraw pupils from the classroom for extra help which bears little or no relationship to what the rest of the class is doing. In the 1970s and early 1980s the most common provision was in a full-time class, which acted as a kind of bottom stream. By the 1990s this had largely given way to withdrawal from selected lessons, but many of the same objections remained.

4. By focusing on differences we remove the perhaps uncomfortable necessity to recognise what children have in common, and hence to review our teaching methods and classroom organisation, to consider how we can cater for the *similarities* between them as much as for the differences.

Conflicts between aims?

Helping children achieve their 'full potential' is an explicit aim in most school prospectuses and staff handbooks. Since this apparently uncontroversial aim is so ubiquitous, it is interesting that the Conservative government of the 1980s was so vocal in denouncing the alleged underachievement of academically less able pupils. Indeed, at the height of the worst recession since the 1930s the Secretary of State was able to secure funds to launch the 'Lower Attaining Pupil Programme' (Joseph, 1983), a stunningly uninspired title which could only have been dreamed up by a civil servant or by a politician with no expectation that the beneficiaries would ever consider voting for his party.

At least since the 1944 Education Act teachers have insisted on the intrinsically worthwhile nature of education. Obviously, it is important to prepare children for their junior or secondary school, but the real purpose of education is to give them intrinsically worthwhile experiences *now*. During the 1980s this liberal view of the aims of education came under attack. Education was increasingly seen as an instrument of government policy, with an emphasis on teachers' responsibility for equipping pupils with the knowledge, skills and attitudes that would enable them to meet the changing demands of the labour market and to play a 'responsible' role in society.

While at first it appeared that secondary schools were the principal target of attack, it soon became clear that primary schools were also included.[1] In both sectors the curriculum underwent substantial changes with an increasing emphasis on science and technology and, in secondary schools, the compulsory teaching of a modern foreign language across the full age and ability range. At the same time work experience became an integral part of the secondary curriculum, and open enrolment legislation[2] required schools to polish up their public image in previously unheard of ways.

The consultations that took place before the 1988 Act was laid before Parliament showed massive professional opposition (Haviland, 1988). Teachers clearly not only disliked the proposals in the Act, but also mistrusted the government's increasingly instrumentalist approach to education. They argued:

1. that the national testing programme associated with the National Curriculum would label large numbers of children as failures from the age of 7;
2. that pressure of national testing would lead to selection within schools, with the best teachers being allocated to the classes whose examination results could be expected to bring credit to the school;
3. that giving parents greater freedom to choose their child's school would create ghetto schools of disadvantaged pupils, especially in urban areas in which parents could not afford to send their children to more privileged schools in the proverbial leafy suburbs;
4. that grant-maintained schools would further accelerate this process;
5. that under local financial management of schools, head teachers and governors would be unwilling to allocate funds to pupils with exceptional needs.

Thus, the objections to the innovations of the 1980s were based largely on the assumption that they would accentuate divisions within the school system and increase the pressure on teachers to differentiate between children in educationally and socially undesirable ways. Far from helping teachers to meet children's needs the Acts of 1980, 1986 and 1988 would make it virtually impossible for teachers to avoid creating additional needs.

These objections raise two issues. First, it is not yet clear whether the 1988 Act will result in discrimination against disadvantaged pupils. Elsewhere I have argued with tongue only partly in cheek that it could be seen as a Marxist measure (Galloway, 1990c). Secondly, it is not at all clear that the rhetoric of the liberal view of education was ever justified. This rhetoric was derived from the dominant individualistic value system of teaching and educational psychology. It claimed to help all pupils achieve their full potential; by concentrating on the individual's needs, potentially destructive comparisons between children could be avoided. This view deserves closer attention.

Why do children fail, and is it inevitable?

We cannot fail at a task unless we have set out to complete it. We may set ourselves the task, or have been set it by someone else. The effect of failure depends on how it is perceived by the child, peers, teachers and other people such as parents. By the time they reach secondary school, children have learned that some tasks are valued more highly than others. Not many secondary pupils are referred to educational psychologists because of their teachers' and parents' deep concern about their progress in art, drama, music or PE. Lack of progress in reading and mathematics is a different matter altogether. Whether lack of success or, more bluntly, failure, matters, depends largely on the status of the task.[3]

Consider two children, William and Joanne, starting at their new secondary school. In the previous six years of primary schooling they have become socialised into the routine of the classroom. Part of this socialisation process was the recognition that some tasks were considered more important than others. It was a gradual process, but an inexorable one. William noticed that his teacher was pleased with his paintings, but concerned about his lack of interest in maths. Joanne noticed that everyone was enthusiastic about her singing and enjoyment of music, but worried about her lack of progress in reading. Over a period of years, both children realised that their lack of progress in these core subjects appeared more important both to their teachers and to their parents than other children's difficulties with painting or music.

This is the process to which sociologists are referring when they say that the status of knowledge is 'socially created'. What neither

William nor Joanne can know is that the status accorded different forms of knowledge varies over time. Difficulties with reading and mathematics still attract more concern than any other curriculum area, but ability in the creative arts is probably valued more highly today than it would have been in the 1930s, or even 1950s. Similarly, oral skills are valued more highly in 1990 than was the case as little as ten years earlier. They are examined in GCSE English Language and play a central part in the modern languages curriculum.

Children's awareness of the importance of different tasks develops as part of their socialisation in the home, and continues at school. By the time they start school at age 5 they have 'learned' gender-specific roles; part of this learning is that boys need some skills more than girls, and vice versa. We may accept that this learning occurs and even welcome it, or we may deplore it and do everything possible to counteract it, but the evidence that it takes place is hardly contentious. Similarly, children in families with a lot of books will have learned the importance, and probably enjoyment, of reading, while others will have had little experience with books but may have developed skills in working with tools and making things.

It follows that some tasks at school may appear more relevant to a child than others. This becomes a problem when the tasks the teacher considers important are felt by the child to be unimportant. By the time they reach their secondary school, children have had six years to discover what their teachers and their parents consider important. They have developed powers of 'metaperception', or the ability to recognise what other people think about them. This can have unfortunate consequences as when children live down to the expectation of a parent or teacher that they are 'not as quick' as an older brother or sister.

Although what counts as high status is culturally determined, the existence of status is evident in all cultures. Whether it is conferred by birth, by membership of a particular tribe or caste, by possession of certain kinds of knowledge or skill, by sporting or literary prowess or by acquired wealth will depend on the dominant values held in society at a given stage in its history. The idea of total equality is naive. Irrespective of the dominant ideology, certain individuals and groups have the power to make decisions affecting the lives of others. Indeed, if this were not the case there would be anarchy.

We seem to be reaching a depressingly gloomy conclusion that some pupils must inevitably be disadvantaged by low status. So far, however, we have skated over a distinction which suggests a way round this problem. Power and status are not synonymous. In Britain the royal family has high status, but very little real power. Estate agents have the power which comes from financial wealth but repeated surveys show that they are not highly regarded by the public at large. The same may apply to accountants and to politicians in local government. One aim of the so-called Thatcherite revolution of the 1980s was to change the public perception of the creation of wealth. Many people came to regard this as morally desirable, if not to be flaunted, and not, like sex to the Victorians, nasty but necessary with any enjoyment well hidden.

Teachers can do little to influence the importance parents attach to different areas of the curriculum. They can do even less to influence the occupations which bestow power and/or prestige. Yet the fact that power and prestige are *not* the same suggests that teachers *do* have some scope for defining what is morally desirable and worth while. A practical example is seen in children's annual reports which distinguish between effort and attainment. There is no logical reason preventing teachers attaching as much value to artistic as to literary acievement nor in preventing them from valuing the achievements of their academically least able pupils as highly as those of the most able.

Yet we should not underestimate the cultural pressures against such high-sounding rhetoric. The senior teacher in charge of the first three years in a large secondary school may be able to show publicly that he or she values the effective teamwork between subject teachers and special needs specialists in teaching two sight-impaired children who have just arrived in Britain from Pakistan as highly as their work with children with no obvious special needs. As long as the local parents are satisfied with their own children's progress, they may well take pleasure and pride that children with handicaps are also doing well. Cultural pressures increase though as adolescence progresses. Some secondary heads might in theory like to say that they value the achievement of a teacher in helping children with severe and complex difficulties to learn to read as highly as that of another teacher in helping three or four pupils win places at Oxbridge. It would be an unusual head who would state this publicly, let alone convince parents and colleagues that he or she really believed it.

Family, school and social class influences on children's educational development

Until the mid-1960s it was widely assumed that family background had an overwhelming influence on children's progress at school.[4] The National Child Development Study followed all children born between the third and ninth of March, 1958 (Wedge and Prosser, 1973; Wedge and Essen, 1982). Children were defined as disadvantaged when their families:

(1) had only one parent and/or five or more children; and/or
(2) lived in an overcrowded house or a house with no hot water; and/or
(3) received means-tested welfare benefits because of their low income.

The study found a strong and consistent relationship between family disadvantage and low attainment at school. More worrying still, this relationship became more marked as the children grew older.

Other research has similarly emphasised the impact of family factors on pupils' development. Rutter (1966), for example, noted the effect of parental ill-health, and in particular psychiatric ill-health. Galloway (1985a) found a very high rate of social disadvantage, combined in many cases with evidence of psychiatric problems, in families of children who were persistently absent from school. Conversely, children from stable, achievement-orientated families start school with the dual advantages that teachers see their parents as cooperative and also that their parents are able to reinforce at home what they do in school.

There is little doubt, then, that family background exerts an important influence on pupils' progress and adjustment at school. This view lay behind the recommendation of the Plowden Committee on primary education to set up educational priority areas (CACE, 1967). Accepting advice from educationalists and psychologists, the committee believed that a child's progress and social development depended on intelligence, personality and family background. Little could be done about any of these. Moreover, the evidence at the time suggested that individual schools made little difference to their pupils' life chances. How a child got on would depend on constitutional and family factors, not on the school's own policy and practice.

Certainly, we cannot ignore the influence of family and community factors on children's educational achievements. Pupils attending inner city schools appear particularly vulnerable (Training Agency, 1990). Nevertheless it should be recognised that this is an oversimplification, since schools are not all equally effective. Reynolds (1976) and Reynolds and Murgatroyd (1977) claimed that secondary modern schools in a Welsh mining valley varied in both the delinquency rates and the attendance of their pupils. More important, they claimed that the differences could not be attributed to differences in the social backgrounds of the pupils they admitted. By far the most influential study of secondary school effectiveness in Britain is the work of Rutter *et al.* (1979). They studied twelve London secondary schools and their effects on pupils. The results showed that a pupil's examination results, attendance, chances of getting into trouble with the police and behaviour within the school were all influenced by the school they attended as well as by their social background. More recently Smith and Tomlinson's (1989) study of multi-racial comprehensives provided strong evidence that the educational progress of ethnic minority pupils was influenced to an important extent by the school they attended. It was no longer possible to attribute pupils' progress, or lack of progress, simply to their social or ethnic background.

It is worth considering why teachers, psychologists and educational researchers had for so long assumed that schools would exert little if any influence on pupils' educational progress and social adjustment independent of their family and social background. The implication of this assumption is extraordinary: namely, that all schools are the same, and that a pupil's progress depends principally on factors over which teachers have no control. Few parents have ever believed this, and estate agents frequently advertise houses as being close to a particularly popular school. The school's influence was probably overlooked for three reasons:

1. Educational psychology was for a long time preoccupied with the assessment of intelligence and personality, largely for the purpose of selecting children for special education or for child guidance clinic treatment. This preoccupation saw problems as being located 'in' a child or family and diverted attention from the quality of teaching provided in school.
2. Sociological research emphasised the influence of social class on children's life chance. Teachers saw themselves as members of a middle-class profession and this research may have reinforced a tendency to underestimate the ability of working-class children (see Tizard *et al.* (1988) for evidence that this is the case).
3. Previous research on differences between schools had concentrated on structural factors such as resources, buildings and school size (e.g. CACE, 1967). It is now clear that these have relatively little impact on a school's overall effectiveness, at least in Britain. The *process* of education appears far more important.[5]

What makes a school effective?

The principal problem with this kind of research is that it is essentially descriptive and atheoretical. Rutter *et al.* (1979) explicitly denied that they could claim a causal relationship between the factors they identified and a school's effectiveness. Thus they found that pot plants were more in evidence at the effective schools than in less effective ones. Does this mean that pot plants contributed to the positive ethos in these schools, or simply that no pot plants would have survived for long in other schools? Were they a cause or an effect of the school's effectiveness? Similarly, Mortimore *et al.* (1988) found the role of the deputy head important in primary schools. Schools in which the deputy was frequently absent or played little active part tended to have lower pupil performance. Again, we have no way of telling why this might have been the case.

A quite different approach to children's progress through their primary and secondary schools has examined the impact of the school on the pupils' development as individuals. Two factors that are central to a person's concept of self are gender and ethnicity. Do schools provide equality for boys and girls and for members of different ethnic groups, or do they accentuate differences?

Other influences on educational development

Gender

Most secondary schools would claim to provide equal opportunities for boys and girls. Many teachers go further and insist, indignantly, that 'we treat them both the same; they both have every opportunity to participate fully in every subject of the curriculum and in extra curricula activities'. Clearly, though, teachers' behaviour towards boys and girls is often not the same. There is extensive evidence that teachers report more boys as disruptive than girls (e.g. Rutter *et al.*, 1970), and there is some evidence from independent observations that boys are more likely to behave in 'difficult' ways than girls (e.g. Tizard *et al.*, 1988). Again, evidence in Britain shows that boys are more frequently backward in reading than girls (e.g. Rutter *et al.*, 1970). More important, perhaps, is the gender bias in choice of subject for GCSE and 'A' levels, with girls under-represented in physics, chemistry and maths, and boys under-represented in biology, the arts and modern languages.[6]

An interesting cross-cultural study suggested that boys may not be at greater risk of reading backwardness than girls in Germany (Preston, 1962). This raises interesting questions about how boys come to be identified as disruptive and about why they are more likely in Britain to have learning difficulties. The claim that boys and girls receive the same treatment and opportunities seldom bears close scrutiny. From the moment they enter school gender-linked differences are emphasised in a whole variety of ways, both covert and overt. In almost all secondary schools boys and girls hang their coats in different places and boys' names are called before girls when taking the register. In many they even sit in different groups for assembly with the threat of being made to sit with the girls (or, less frequently, the boys) a powerful sanction against pupils who misbehave. Even if these activities are integrated, it is hard to imagine any head teacher daring to integrate the toilets.

The organisational differences may have less impact on pupils than the differences in behaviour expected of boys and girls. Since many teachers are parents, it is not surprising that, like parents, they often expect boys to be noisier and more rowdy than girls. A girl who prefers to dress like a boy may attract little comment provided she does not flout her school's uniform rules by refusing to wear a skirt, but a boy who prefers to dress like a girl is often the subject of concern. Behaviour that is labelled 'boisterous' in a boy may be called 'aggressive' in a girl. There is some evidence that teachers tend to attribute girls' failure on a task to lack of ability, whereas boys' failure is more likely to be attributed to lack of effort (Dweck *et al.*, 1978). Taking this argument a stage further, it is possible that behaviour that is seen as 'simple' naughtiness in boys, and capable of control by minor sanctions, may be regarded as evidence of emotional instability in girls.

The point about all these differences is that they are socially created. There is no obvious biological justification for any of them. They have developed in a social context and are maintained socially. Communities differ in the social roles they expect boys and girls, or men and women, to fill. Fundamentalist Christian groups have something in common with fundamentalist Islamic groups in differentiating sharply between the roles of men and women in the family and in society. Consequently they place a high priority on separate schools for boys and girls as a way of socialising them into the sex roles they see as desirable. Other Christian and Islamic groups have different views about the respective responsibilities of men and women in the family and in society, and consequently see the school's task differently.

All this raises a difficult question for teachers in state schools, even if their school is 'controlled' or 'aided' by a religious group. Both teachers and parents will have their own ideas about what sort of behaviour is 'appropriate' for boys and girls. Similarly, they will have ideas about the sort of knowledge and the sort of skills that are important for each sex. They are unlikely, however, to have selected a school either because of their own commitment to a particular view about girls' and boys' education or because of the school's stated policy. Thus, although they will have their own biases, expectations and prejudices, these may be implicit rather than explicit.

Ethnicity

Not all schools have a multi-ethnic pupil intake but all work in a multi-ethnic and multi-cultural society. In the 1960s and 1970s a long, acrimonious and largely futile debate raged over two questions whose educational implications were at best uncertain. The first was whether intelligence was inherited. The second assumed an affirmative answer and considered whether ethnic groups varied in their inherited intelligence. The principal interest in this debate for present purposes lies in what it tells us about psychologists. While many psychologists would like to claim that psychology is the impartial, scientific study of behaviour, the fact remains that they choose both the subjects of study and the methods. To believe that they set out in a disinterested way to discover whether intelligence is or is not inherited is naive. Much more frequently they set out to obtain evidence in support of a particular point of view. This led Sir Cyril Burt, the father of educational psychology in Britain, to publish articles using data that were almost certainly fraudulent (Hearnshaw, 1979). Nor is it often legitimate to claim that psychologists have no control over how politicians or educationists use the scientific evidence they obtain (Kamin, 1974). If you believe that one group of people is genetically superior in intelligence to another, whether the latter group be black, Irish or working class, it is a very short step to supporting a system that offers superior opportunities to the 'superior' group. The logical result is apartheid.

We said earlier that the debate over the inheritance of intelligence was long, acrimonious and largely futile. The futility lay partly in the concept of intelligence and partly in the confusion over the moral uses of the research. What counts as intelligence depends on the culture under investigation. Inevitably, researchers have to adopt a definition consistent with the views of the dominant culture in their society. This leads to the well-known conclusion that intelligence is what intelligence tests measure. As important, it is never possible to be certain that we have adequately taken account of all the variables that may affect a pupil's measured intelligence. The head of a residential 'open-air' school for delicate children once claimed to David Galloway that earlier in his career, in the 1930s, he had demonstrated with the use of controls that pupils' IQ could be raised several points by thawing them out on the hot water pipes a few minutes before testing. Disentangling the complex web of school, family and environmental influences on test performance is infinitely more difficult. Yet these are essentially technical problems. Whether it is worth trying to overcome depends not on their technical difficulty but on the ethical purposes of the research.

In the 1960s and 1970s many ethnic minority groups opposed research programmes which compared their children's performance with that of the white majority. The reason was that they mistrusted the uses to which the white majority would put the research. In other words, they feared that the research would be used to justify their children's low achievements, if not to legitimise discrimination against them. In the 1980s many ethnic minority groups have insisted on monitoring their children's progress, seeing the results as a way of demonstrating inequality of opportunity and demanding better resources. Hence research can never be separated from its perceived moral objectives.

The school's role in creating equal opportunities.

The rhetoric of the late 1980s and 1990s demands equal opportunities for boys and girls. Some religious groups insist that boys and girls should not have the same opportunities since their responsibilities in later life will be *different*. They tend also to insist that provision of *different* opportunities does not mean that they have unequal value. The counter to this is that provision of different opportunities leads almost inevitably to inequality, with girls' education perceived as less important than boys'.

The school's role in a multi-ethnic society raises similar questions. The principle of equality of opportunity is not contentious but its implementation most certainly is. One view holds that schools should celebrate cultural diversity, arguing both that cultural traditions are interdependent and hence that children should learn about each other's cultures, and also that personal identity is strengthened by strong cultural ties. This view holds that schools should recognise and help to maintain children's home languages by appointing teachers who speak them, and in secondary schools offering them as an alternative to European languages for GCSE and 'A' level. This view would also seek to question the high status of 'public' activities, for example in the employment field, compared with 'private' activities predominantly performed by women, such as looking after young children. An alternative view is that schools should see their task principally in terms of education about British culture. Thus, the daily act of worship should generally be Christian in nature and the curriculum should be designed to teach all children about British cultural traditions and history. This essentially assimilationist philosophy is evident in the National Curriculum introduced by the 1988 Education Reform Act. This Act was, of course, a political measure. It contrasts in an interesting way with the dominant professional ideology which still insists on the importance of preparing trainee teachers for work in a multi-ethnic society (DES, 1989a).

We should note a dissenting ethnic minority voice at this stage. The idea that schools should seek to strengthen cultural identity has not gone unchallenged. There are two related arguments. First, the methods that schools use to support cultural identities may be seen as a thinly veiled attempt to legitimise discrimination. Secondly, parents want schools to help them gain the knowledge and skills that will help them in the labour market. Thus Stone's (1981) research indicates that Afro-Caribbean parents were sceptical about the interest their children's teachers took in their contribution to the school's sporting or musical reputation. What parents wanted was 'O' levels. Similarly, Nash (1983) drew attention to the practice in New Zealand schools of encouraging school clubs that promoted awareness of Maori heritage while streaming Maori pupils into low status classes. The clubs, like brass bands and sports teams, could be seen as a way of socialising Maori pupils into accepting inferior status in the schools, and ultimately in society.

All this is somewhat remote from the more obvious evidence of sexism and racism in schools. Some of the most widely publicised examples are in primary schools. It is now some years since the publishers of the Ladybird books dressed Jane in jeans, but sex role stereotyping is still evident in many of the most frequently used reading schemes. In its most extreme form girls help mother with the housework while boys help father dig the garden or wash the car. Similar biases, though, are all too evident in secondary schools. Problems in mathematics books draw disproportionately on male characters. History often presents a white, male, British version of events, with emphasis on war. Children are taught about the Indian mutiny, not the first war of Indian independence. The geography and religious education syllabus, too, can encourage an ethnocentric perspective, seeing other countries and other religions from an anglo-centric perspective. The curriculum, then, can all too easily become the mode through which the beliefs, values and prejudices of the dominant culture are transmitted. When these beliefs, values and prejudices conflict with or devalue those of other cultures, implicitly or explicitly, the education system becomes the means whereby inequality is maintained and perhaps made more extreme.

This can be seen as 'institutionalised' sexism and racism. It is institutionalised in the sense that it arises from the unconscious assimilation of attitudes as a result of teachers' own socialisation, not from a conscious intent to discriminate against any particular group. Research by psychologists can help teachers to become more aware of their own attitudes and of the effect their classroom behaviour has on children's self-esteem or motivation. Research by psychologists can also provide evidence that is interpreted as legitimising existing attitudes and behaviour. Psychology, then *can* be an instrument of social control. However, it can also be an instrument of change, helping teachers to explore ways of understanding their pupils and evaluating their own work as teachers. The same, of course, applies to sociology, philosophy and the study of history.

Individual or group differences?

Differences in gender, social class and ethnicity all refer to membership of identified groups. The relevance of this for teachers claiming to meet individual needs is that a sense of personal or individual identity arises in a social context. By the time they start school, children's gender identity is well established, but how their concept of gender develops will be affected by their socialisation at school as well as at home. A school's equal opportunities policy may be reflected in the curriculum, in the relationships between teachers and children, and also in the relationship between teachers. In this case children may learn that responsibility is awarded according to ability rather than gender and that gender has little relevance to their educational progress through the curriculum. Alternatively, the hidden messages conveyed through the curriculum and through interpersonal relationships in the school may be that decision making is a male preserve, at least in important matters, and that day-to-day activities are determined by gender rather than interest or ability.

To feel secure children, and adults, need to feel that they are members of a group. This was a recurring theme in the work of Emile Dürkheim (1858–1917), one of the 'fathers' of educational sociology (e.g. Dürkheim, 1952). Over 90 years ago Dürkheim was writing about the importance of a sense of social cohesiveness, or solidarity. More recently Hargreaves (1982) argued that the 'cult of individualism' that pervades the British school system consistently underestimates the importance of a sense of group solidarity. Hargreaves was writing about secondary schools. He argued that when pupils feel they have little chance of achieving success in the school's official activities they protect their self-esteem by identifying with other similarly disaffected pupils, and develop a group identity which depends on rejection of the school's aims and values.

Hargreaves' principal interest was in the formation of 'counter-cultures' on which certain pupils maintain their self-respect by jointly rejecting the school's aims and values. This is evident in its most extreme form in the final two years of compulsory education. Its origins, though, are evident from the start of secondary schooling, and even in primary schools. It is seen when children obtain social recognition from other children as well, incidentally, as their teacher's attention, for deliberately noisy behaviour or for failing to follow instructions. It is seen in the 12 year-old whose sense of personal identity is maintained by his reputation as clown of the class. It is seen in the girl whose reputation for absentmindedness has become a standard joke in her class, as well as in her family.

We cannot, then, hope to understand individual differences simply by studying individual pupils. Children's behaviour and achievements have to be seen in social context. Consequently, we need to ask whether this context reduces the educational impact of differences between children or serves to increase them.

Conclusions: similarities or differences?

How far, then, does psychology help teachers to understand the differences between children? It is easy to give examples of research with obvious implications for teachers. Cross-cultural research, for example, illustrates the importance of differences in conventions about verbal and non-verbal behaviour. A classic example is eye contact. In many cultures, including the majority culture in Britain, a child's failure to make eye contact when talking to an authority figure is seen as 'shiftiness' or even insolence. In other cultures it would be insolent for a child to make eye contact with an elder, especially in a disciplinary situation. Teachers should clearly recognise situations in which verbal or non-verbal behaviour is likely to be misinterpreted.[7]

Yet examples of psychological research with immediate applications for teachers avoid a more important and more general question about differences between children. The central problem is best illustrated in the work on the inheritance of intelligence and in the development of normative tests. Briefly, the ideology of the person doing the research, or using the tests, is likely to influence the uses to which the results are put. As the study of behaviour, psychology is value free, yet the mere fact of studying behaviour tells us nothing about the researcher's motivation and methods, nor about the uses to which he or she hopes to put the results. Thus the ideas of psychologists are not value free. Psychology offers a variety of methodologies for investigating educational problems. The problem may be how to teach *all* pupils more effectively, though in this case the researcher would have to make a moral and political judgement as to what counts as 'effective' education. Alternatively the problem may be how to identify 10–20 per cent of pupils for a privileged education leading to lucrative high-status jobs, as when children were separated at the age of 11 for a grammar school place. Psychology can help to create equality of opportunity, or to discriminate against particular groups.

Traditionally, educational psychology in Britain has been concerned with what distinguishes one pupil from another rather than with what they have in common. Indeed, differences could be described as the *raison d'être* of applied educational psychologists. The perceived ability of educational psychologists to identify the sources of individual differences and to discuss the educational implications constitutes a large part of their professional identity. Nevertheless, it is highly problematic. If provision of equal opportunities means anything it presumably means that factors such as social class, gender and race are not the basis for offering pupils qualitatively different experiences in school.

The problem with this view is that some pupils have exceptional difficulty with all or parts of the curriculum. Others have, or present, behavioural problems. A legitimate argument is that children need to learn what they have in common with their peers, but this learning can only take place if the educationally significant differences between them are recognised. The curriculum, then, must differentiate between children's different needs. This 'liberal' perspective provides an obvious role for educational psychologists in helping teachers to recognise and meet individual needs. An alternative perspective sees learning and behaviour difficulties as threatening teachers' need for control and hence their self-esteem. Here the educational psychologist's role could still lie in helping teachers to recognise and meet individual needs, but it could also be seen in terms of social control, with the emphasis on identifying problem children in order to remove them from the classroom or, at least, to suggest ways of reducing the difficulties they present. Either perspective leads to a consideration of special educational needs.

Notes and further reading

1. For example, primary schools were criticised both by Ministers and by HMI, for the alleged lack of 'rigour' in their approach to the curriculum. One of the government's responses to this was to require all primary PGCE and BEd. courses to provide the basis on which each student would build the expertise needed to provide leadership in one area of the curriculum.
2. Parents' rights to choose their children's school were greatly increased in the Education Acts of 1980 and 1988. The only legal grounds on which a child may be refused a place in a LEA-maintained school is now lack of space.
3. The most significant contributions to understanding the status of different forms of knowledge have been made by educational sociologists, for example Bourdieu (1977).
4. There is an extensive literature on the relationship between social disadvantage and educational progress. Two books have been particularly influential: Rutter and Madge (1976) and Mortimore and Blackstone (1982).
5. For reviews of research on school effectiveness, see Galloway (1985b) and Reynolds (1985) and (1991).
6. For evidence on gender differences in subject choice, see Griffin (1991). For a critique of gender and social class issues, see Deem (1986).
7. For a review of cross-cultural differences in non-verbal communication, see Vogelaar and Silverman (1984). A fascinating study from New Zealand is provided by Metge and Kinloch (1978).

Seminar suggestions

1. List the ways in which boys and girls are treated differently in the course of a typical day at the school you know best. Does this different treatment matter? What do children learn from it?
2. As you enter the classroom you hear one child calling another a 'black sod'. What do you do?
3. In what ways do you think schools can best mitigate the effects of social disadvantage?

CHAPTER 3

Special educational needs

Introduction

Which children are we talking about?

As Secretary of State for Education and Science, Margaret Thatcher in 1974 appointed Mary Warnock to chair a committee:

to review educational provision in England, Scotland and Wales for children and young people handicapped by disabilities of body or mind, taking account of the medical aspects of their needs, together with arrangements to prepare them for entering into employment; to consider the most effective use of resources; and to make recommendations.

The Committee published its report four years later (DES, 1978a). At this time roughly 2 per cent of children nationally were being educated in special schools or special classes. Other children with learning difficulties were taught in the remedial departments of mainstream secondary schools or, in primary schools, by remedial teachers who were often employed part time. Almost all such help was based on removing the child from the mainstream classroom.

Special schools catered for the eleven categories of handicap recognised under the 1944 Education Act in the mistaken belief that a category of *medical* handicap could define the nature of a child's *educational* needs; some children in wheelchairs are able to benefit from the full range of the National Curriculum without special educational help, whereas children with a relatively minor but permanent injury to their writing hand may require specialised resources, at least in the short to medium term.

The Warnock Report recommended abolition of the categories recognised under the 1944 Act, replacing them with the generic concept of special educational need. This referred to children with learning difficulties that might be mild, moderate or severe. It was expected that schools would normally be able to cater for children with mild learning difficulties without additional resources, whereas children with moderate and severe learning difficulties would normally require multi-disciplinary assessment to identify their needs and determine the additional help required to meet them.

Perhaps the most well known of Warnock's conclusions was that up to 15 per cent of children would require some form of special educational help at any one time, and up to 20 per cent at some stage of their school careers. Special educational needs, therefore, were seen as a responsibility for *all* teachers. In the same year, HMI in Scotland published an influential report arguing that at least 50 per cent of children could be said to have learning difficulties, and that mainstream schools should accept responsibility for them (SED, 1978).

The research on which the Warnock Committee based its conclusions was carried out by psychologists, child psychiatrists and community health specialists (e.g. Rutter *et al.*, 1975; Davie *et al.*, 1972). It described the prevalence of learning and behavioural difficulties among children of different ages. Yet while claiming to be based on solid research evidence, Warnock's conclusion was a political compromise based on a moral judgement. The research was based largely on children's results in intelligence and reading tests and on behaviour rating scales completed by parents and teachers. Intelligence and reading tests are designed to distinguish between children of differing ability. The behaviour rating scales contained items that were familiar to teachers, on the reasonable grounds that the research was investigating problems of immediate relevance to teachers. The design of the instruments ensured that a large minority of children could be identified as having, or presenting, problems. Any committee could use the results to identify an entirely arbitrary proportion of children as having special needs, 5, 10, 20, 30 or 50 per cent, and claim respectable research evidence in support of their conclusion. To have identified only 5 per cent of children as having special needs would have left the committee open to the charge that they simply had not recognised the range and complexity of problems facing teachers in mainstream schools. To have identified 50 per cent, like HMI in Scotland (SED, 1978), would have invited ridicule from the government as unrealistic. Twenty per cent was a convenient political compromise. It was also a moral judgement, implying that teachers *ought* to be able to cater for roughly 80 per cent of their pupils without extra help, but that the most problematic 20 per cent *ought* to receive particular attention.

What do children with special educational needs have in common?

Among children with physical and sensory impairment, and children with severe intellectual handicap, there is a relatively even social class distribution. In other words, professional parents are about as likely to have children with these difficulties as working-class parents. In the case of children identified as having emotional and behavioural difficulties this is not the case. They are much more likely to come from manual working-class families. The same applies to children with mild learning difficulties in mainstream schools and to children with moderate learning difficulties,who could be regarded as having a moderate level of intellectual impairment, in special schools.

Children with mild and moderate learning difficulties and/or emotional and behavioural difficulties constitute a majority of the 20 per cent Warnock regarded as having special educational needs. As well as coming predominantly from manual working-class homes, these groups contain a disproportionate number of boys – between two and three boys for every girl – and also a disproportionate number of children from ethnic minority groups. The common element in learning and behavioural difficulties is that teachers find the children's progress and/or behaviour disturbing. The social class, ethnic and gender bias suggest that identification of special needs may be based as much on the teacher's need for stability in the classroom as on the child's need for special help. This suggestion is supported by consistent evidence that children's educational progress is no better at special schools than at mainstream schools (e.g. Carlberg and Kavale, 1980; Galloway and Goodwin, 1987). Hence, provision for special educational needs raises ethical questions as well as practical ones of school and classroom organisation.[1]

Ethical issues

We cannot need something without in some sense also wanting it (see pp. 6–11). Learning and behavioural problems at school are usually identified by teachers. In identifying a child as having special educational needs teachers may be drawing attention to their concern about:

(1) the child;
(2) the effect the child is having on the progress or the behaviour of other children in the class;
(3) the inadequacy of the resources available within the classroom;
(4) the effect of the child's presence on their own job-satisfaction and sense of personal well-being.

None of these, of course, is exclusive of the others. They do nevertheless illustrate two crucial points. First, we cannot usefully think about children with special needs in isolation from the school and classroom context in which these needs are apparent. Secondly, the needs of children and the needs of teachers are inter-related. Attempting to focus on the child's needs alone, for example by means of individual intelligence or personality assessment, individualises the problem by pretending that other factors, such as social interaction within the classroom, the teacher's experience and ability or the availability of appropriate resources are irrelevant. Bluntly, it makes the child responsible for any short-comings that may lie within the school or classroom.

Equal opportunities

The Warnock Report was adamant that special educational needs was a relative concept, not an absolute one. Whether or not a child was considered to have special needs would depend on the circumstances, not simply on any supposedly scientific measure of personality or intelligence. It is doubtful, however, whether the committee fully recognised the implications of its own position. The report emphasised the differences between children with special needs and other children, and never got to grips with ways in which schools might contribute to pupils' difficulties. Nor did the report ever get to grips with the moral question of pupils' entitlement to participate in activities available to other children. These issues were identified a great deal more clearly in the report of a committee chaired by John Fish, a former HMI, for the Inner London Education Authority (ILEA, 1985). This committee was clear that:

The aims of education for children and young people with disabilities and significant handicaps are the same as those for all children and young people. They should have opportunities to achieve these aims and to associate with their contemporaries, whether similarly disabled or not, and have access to the whole range of opportunities in education, training, leisure and community activities available to all. Disabilities and significant difficulties do not diminish the right to equal access to, and participation in, society. (Para. 1.1.22)

This insistence on equal opportunities for pupils with special needs contained both a moral and a political statement. The former is self-evident. The latter reflected the concern of elected members on the Inner London Education Committee that the school system was currently offering unequal and implicitly inferior opportunities to working-class children and to members of ethnic minority groups. Gender was also a concern of the committee, and the over-representation of boys in schools for children with learning and behavioural difficulties was relevant here. Taking the argument a step further, the report maintained that 'children and young people may have the handicapping effects of their disabilities increased by social factors and educational experiences' (Para. 1.1.36).

From here it was a short step to the conclusion that: 'Meeting special educational needs is an integral aspect of education for all' (Para. 1.1.45).

Responses to special educational needs

A deficit model

Advice from psychologists, notably Sir Cyril Burt, had been influential in the decision in the 1944 Education Act to adopt a tripartite system of grammar, technical and secondary modern schools. However, the Act assumed that some children would not fit into this system. These children would have to be identified and 'special' education provided for them. Psychologists who claimed a 'scientific' basis for selecting children for grammar schools could make a similar claim in selecting children for special schools. Under the Act school medical officers were able to 'ascertain' a child as suffering from one of ten handicapping conditions. As there were insufficient educational psychologists to carry out the necessary assessments, doctors were trained to administer intelligence tests, and these formed the basis for ascertainment as 'educationally subnormal'. As educational psychologists gradually became more numerous, they claimed expertise in identifying educational needs, arguing that doctors should stick to the implications for teachers of any relevant medical conditions. This trend culminated in the 1981 Education Act which imposed on all LEAs an obligation to obtain an educational psychologist's report, together with reports from teachers and school medical officers, as part of a multi-disciplinary assessment of a child's special educational needs.

The emphasis, though, remained on identifying the special needs of individual pupils and on production of a 'statement' setting out how the LEA intended to meet these needs. The 1981 Act is responsible for the dreadful neologism 'statemented children' becoming educational jargon in Britain.[2] The model, then, remained a deficit one. In practice, if not necessarily in theory, the problem was still seen as finding remedies for the deficits, or difficulties of individual children. Psychological tests had always claimed to identify current functioning. Their claims to predict future performance had been made with considerable confidence until research showed that children's IQ could change substantially within two or three years (e.g. Hindley and Owen, 1978). Teachers, administrators and many educational psychologists nevertheless continued to rely on them.

Yet the deficit model with its primary emphasis on fitting the child into the system, as opposed to analysing the system to see why it was failing to meet the child's needs, was inappropriate both in theory and in practice. The practical problem was that if as many as 20 per cent of children had special needs, let alone the 50 per cent identified by HMI in Scotland (SED, 1978), then responses must be institutional rather than individual. With classes of up to 30, and in some LEAs 35, teachers have limited time to design individual programmes for children, let alone put them into practice. The aim, therefore, must be to help individuals through class or group activities. The theoretical problem is that children's personal and educational development takes place, for better or worse, in social contexts. Hence, if we are serious about enhancing opportunities for personal and educational development, we must have regard to the quality of the child's experience as a member of a class. Observation of children, whether they have special needs or not, shows that they learn from each other. Indeed, the quality of learning experiences depends to a considerable extent on how far a teacher organises activities to make this possible. Attempts to select individual children for extra help or withdrawal groups largely ignores these problems.

Support for learning within a whole school approach to special educational needs

The argument presented so far implies that schools will not cater effectively for pupils with special needs on a piece-meal basis in which special provision is bolted on to what is provided for the majority of pupils. Rather, provision for the majority has to be sufficiently flexible to accommodate pupils with special needs. This is the essential feature of a whole school approach. It acknowledges the possibility that the school's organisation, curriculum, teaching methods and provision for pupil welfare may be contributing to pupil's difficulties rather than meeting them. Simmons (1986, p.19) identified three characteristics of a whole school approach. It should ensure:

(a) that *all* teachers, not just those primarily concerned with special needs, should be aware of the range of needs that might arise in their classrooms;
(b) that *all* teachers should be responsible for assessing the difficulties of material used in their lessons; and
(c) that *all* teachers should have access to specialised help in dealing, inside the classroom, with children with learning difficulties.

It is worth noting that the DES (1988b) seems to share this view. In a circular letter to all higher education institutions involved in INSET provision, the DES asserted that training for teachers with designated responsibility for meeting special needs in ordinary schools should help them in:

identifying impediments to pupils' learning and devising strategies to overcome them;
considering the implications, *for the curriculum and full life* of the school as a whole, of the presence of children with a range of special educational needs;

implementing appropriate forms of organisation for the additional and supplementary help which will *give such children access to the full range of the curriculum.* (DES, 1988b, p.5: our italics).

Our only reservation about the criteria of Simmons and the DES is that the changing approach to special educational needs requires explicit attention to the rights and responsiblities of pupils as well as to what is expected of teachers. In particular, three issues have recurred when we have explored the concept of special educational need on INSET courses:

(a) that *all* pupils should have access to the full range of the curriculum;
(b) that *all* pupils should have the opportunity, be expected and be seen to contribute usefully to the life and work of the school;
(c) that *all* pupils, irrespective of ability, should be encouraged and expected to develop an awareness of, and respect for, individual differences.

The first of these requires further comment. The National Curriculum has to be accessible to all pupils, unless a statement of their special needs exempts them from part or all of its requirements. In addition, head teachers can exempt pupils on a temporary basis in certain quite strictly specified circumstances (see DES, 1989b). Yet the fact that children with severe or complex difficulties cannot reasonably be expected to meet the attainment targets for their age group does not mean that the whole curriculum area is inappropriate. The 1988 Education Reform Act insisted not only that the National Curriculum applies to the large majority of pupils with special needs, but also that exemption can only be granted in restricted circumstances, and then only if alternative curricular arrangements are stated. This may do more to stimulate constructive thought about the curriculum for pupils with special needs than the Warnock Report and the 1981 Education Act put together.[3]

Models of support

Until the late 1980s, the most frequent form of support for children with special needs in secondary schools was to remove them from the classroom for extra help with reading or, less frequently, mathematics. A popular alternative in the 1970s was to create a full-time class, so that children spent all their time in the 'remedial' department. In the early 1980s this model of provision attracted increasing criticism from HMI. The inspectorate argued that full-time remedial classes provided an undesirably restricted curriculum, and were socially divisive. The 1988 Education Reform Act, with its emphasis on a specified curricular entitlement for virtually all pupils, finally persuaded most head teachers that the full-time class was no longer viable.

The National Curriculum meant that pupils with special needs could no longer be the sole responsibility of special needs teachers. Because they were entitled to the full range of the curriculum, they must be taught in subject departments and their teachers must have support from specialist colleagues in reorganising and meeting their needs. Hence, the emphasis was switching away from withdrawal groups for extra help in maths and English to support within the ordinary class.

This principle is not accepted in all schools. Some heads and some special needs teachers continue to base most of the school's provision on withdrawal groups. Moreover, this approach is implicitly encouraged in many LEAs by peripatetic reading and language services which see their task as working with individuals or small groups. In some LEAs additional provision for pupils with statements consists almost entirely of individual help for up to one-fifth of the week from a member of a central service. A good deal of research has been carried out on the effectiveness of this kind of 'remedial' teaching (e.g. Sampson, 1975; Tobin and Pumfrey, 1976). The evidence suggests that children tend to make quite good progress while attending remedial groups, but that this progress is unlikely to be maintained when they return full time to their regular classes.

On theoretical grounds this is only to be expected. Social learning theory emphasises the importance of context in people's behaviour.[4] Skills that children learn in one context will not necessarily transfer to another unless they are consciously practised in the new context. This indicates the most common problem with withdrawal groups. There is seldom time for meetings that might enable withdrawal group teachers to base their activities on work that the rest of the class would be doing. Consequently the remedial work often bears little relationship to the children's regular classroom experience. This means: (a) that they receive no direct help with the activities they find difficult; (b) that on return to the classroom they have little opportunity to consolidate the skills they have learned in the remedial group, since the rest of the class is following entirely different activities; (c) that class teachers receive little or no practical guidance on how they might be able to help children with learning difficulties, since responsibility lies with the remedial specialist.

A whole school approach to special needs aims to overcome these problems by giving children, and subject teachers, support within the ordinary classroom. The form this support takes can vary widely, depending on the needs both of the children and of their teachers. It can include:

(1) planning units of work to enable *all* children to take part in an active way;

(2) the special needs teacher working with an individual or with a group of children with learning difficulties;
(3) the specialist teacher working temporarily with the majority of the class, releasing the class teacher to work with children with special needs;
(4) planning assessment, monitoring and record-keeping procedures;
(5) planning and implementing programmes to tackle 'difficult' behaviour in individuals or groups;
(6) assessing the readability level of materials in daily use in the classroom.

In theory, providing help within the ordinary class overcomes the problems of learning transfer that bedevilled remedial withdrawal groups, while at the same time developing the class teacher's own skills in recognising special needs and responding to them. In practice, formidable problems still arise. Although many LEAs have asked all head teachers to identify a coordinator with responsibility for special needs provision, staffing constraints mean that few subject teachers can expect a great deal of in-class support. Also, the relationship between class teachers and a specialist colleague working alongside them is unfortunately not always an easy one. The specialist's suggestions can be interpreted as criticism and her or his presence perceived as a threat to the class teacher's autonomy.[5]

Future trends in light of the 1988 Education Reform Act

The 1988 Education Reform Act introduced local management of schools to all secondary schools. This meant that governors were given responsibility for staffing, subject to their annual budget. In most LEAs the annual budget is based on pupil numbers, supplemented by an additional weighting intended to reflect factors such as social disadvantage in the pupil intake or the number of pupils with special needs. It is important to recognise that this additional part of the annual budget cannot be earmarked for the pupils concerned. How it is spent is up to the school, though local inspectors and HMI are able to bring pressure to bear if they feel that a school is neglecting its responsibilities to certain pupils.

A further point is that resources for children with a statement of their special needs may be funded centrally by the LEA, and not form part of the budget delegated to schools. This could lead some head teachers to refer an increasing number of children for formal assessment in order (a) to obtain additional resources that the school could not otherwise afford, and (b) to obtain the child's exemption from some or all of the requirements of the National Curriculum.

Whether this happens will depend largely on the clarity and

consistency of LEA policies on statementing. It is worth repeating, though, that the 1988 Act may have done more to stimulate discussion about the curriculum for children with special needs than the 1981 Act. The National Curriculum can only be dis-applied or modified in highly specific circumstances (DES, 1989b). Moreover, schools will be judged by their pupils' performance in the national testing programmes at ages 7, 11, 14 and 16. It follows that schools will have to give serious thought to the effectiveness of their provision for the less able 20, 40 or 50 per cent of their pupils. Schools which concentrate on a small élite of pupils, as in the days of the 11+, may find it difficult to conceal from parents the inadequacy of provision for academically less able children.

With recognition that all teachers have responsibility for special needs, the organisation of support within the school is attracting increasing attention. Not all subject specialists welcome an obligation to teach children who might previously have been taught in remedial classes. A whole-school policy requires that the head of special needs has the explicit support of the school's senior management. It is often helpful if a deputy head is nominated as coordinator for special needs, with responsibility for ensuring that the school's policy is adopted in every subject department.

Currently many special needs teachers in secondary schools work directly with subject teacher colleagues in providing support for children with special needs. The obvious problem here is that the special needs teacher may have no specific expertise in, say, science, yet has to help a colleague find ways to make the science syllabus accessible and enjoyable for children with a range of learning and behavioural difficulties. The special needs teacher should have expertise in developing materials suitable for children with varying abilities, but will not necessarily have particular expertise in the area with which the child, or class teacher, is having problems. It follows that special needs coordinators may find they can use their expertise more effectively by working with a designated teacher in each subject department rather than directly with class teachers. For example, the science teacher with responsibility for special needs would then be able to help colleagues adapt their class programme in the light of the children's needs. Subject departments, therefore, would have responsibility for the full range of needs within their own curriculum area, with the special needs teacher acting as a consultant when difficulties arose.

Children with more complex or severe difficulties

We are referring here to children with difficulties which call for additional resources to those routinely available in mainstream schools. These can take many forms including severe intellectual handicap, physical impairment, visual or auditory impairment or speech and communication difficulties. Children with moderate levels of intellectual handicap and children with severe emotional and behavioural difficulties can also present substantial learning and management problems in ordinary classes, calling for some kind of additional support. Under the 1944 Act children with these more complex or severe difficulties were 'ascertained' as suffering from a category of handicap and the LEA was obliged to place them in a special school or class catering for the category in question. Educational psychologists and school medical officers cooperated, and sometimes competed, in identifying children for the available facilities.

This raises some interesting questions about the role of educational psychologists and about the use to which educational psychology is put. Superficially, the expansion of special schools following the 1944 Act could be seen as a logical extension to the tripartite system of grammar, technical and secondary modern schools. However, it can also be seen as a logical extension to the institutions for mentally handicapped people that had proliferated in the Victorian and post-Victorian era.

Special schools and institutional provision for handicapped adults can be seen in two lights. A conventional view sees such provision as a benevolently humanitarian attempt to cater for people needing specialised forms of care, treatment or teaching. A more cynical view sees them as an attempt to remove from circulation people whose presence poses a threat to the stability of society. Members of the eugenics movement advocated life-long segregation of the mentally retarded on the grounds that their mental and associated moral degeneracy would create unmanageable problems in and for society. Influential books in the nineteenth century traced the descendants of problem families and claimed high rates of delinquency and sexual promiscuity to be associated with mental deficiency (e.g. Dugdale, 1977). More recently David Galloway remembers an eminent lecturer on his psychology degree course in the late 1960s expressing concern about the fertility of working-class families. Because they bred more rapidly than the middle class, and tended to have a lower IQ, the average intelligence of the nation was likely to fall.[6]

The political nature of this view has been dealt with elsewhere (see Kamin, 1974; and Chapter 8). Its scientific underpinning has also been discredited, not least with the exposure as probably fraudulent of much of Burt's work on the inheritance of intelligence (Hearnshaw, 1979). It is no longer supported in the crude form proposed by the eugenicists, at least openly. Nevertheless, there is still an interesting parallel in school and LEA responses to special educational needs.

Children with learning or behavioural difficulties pose a threat not only to the stability of the classroom, but also to their teacher's self-esteem. In a literal sense they are *disturbing* to teach. This is confirmed by research on stress in teaching which consistently shows teachers reporting learning and behavioural problems as a major source of stress from day-to-day teaching (e.g. Dunham, 1984). The 1988 Education Reform Act introduced national testing programmes with the possibility that publication of the results would lead to highly publicised comparisons between schools. In this context pressure to remove 'misfits' from the mainstream could grow. Although the Warnock Report (DES, 1978a) and the 1981 Education Act are widely believed to have encouraged the integration of children with special needs into mainstream schools, the evidence that this is actually happening is far from clear. Swann's (1985, 1991) analyses of DES statistics showed an increase in the number of children with sensory impairment in mainstream schools. This was not, however, the case with learning difficulties of a 'moderate' nature. For these children, and to a slightly lesser extent for children with emotional and behavioural difficulties, the trend was in the opposite direction, towards increased segregation from the mainstream.

The obvious question is whether this should be a matter for concern. Special schools are designed to meet special needs, so surely they must provide more appropriate teaching? There are two ways of dealing with this question. First, research has quite consistently shown that children tend to make better educational progress in mainstream schools. Several literature reviews have failed to find a single study showing children with moderate learning difficulties making better educational progress in special schools (e.g. Galloway and Goodwin, 1987). Children with physical impairments, too, appear able to make good educational progress in mainstream primary schools (e.g. Anderson, 1973), as do children with hearing impairment (e.g. Lynas, 1985).

The second response is perhaps less straightforward. By definition, special schools that operate in isolation from the mainstream cannot meet certain needs, for example:

(1) the need to learn to play and work with 'non-handicapped' peers;
(2) to develop an understanding of their own abilities *and* difficulties in the context of mainstream expectations;
(3) to receive the 'broad and balanced' curriculum available to children in mainstream schools, including the extra-curricular activities;
(4) to strengthen their sense of being valued members of the local community by attending the school which serves that community.

All these points are based on the value judgement that children with special needs 'ought' to attend their local school and that LEAs 'ought' to provide them, and their teachers, with the resources necessary for this to be successful. Research evidence supports this value judgement but did not give rise to it.

Implications for educational psychologists

Where does all this leave educational psychologists? Psychologists, too, live in and are part of, a social world. The idea that psychologists, or any other scientists, spend their time in the disinterested pursuit of truth is naive. Psychologists were active in the eugenics movement. They believed strongly in the moral justification for their views, and used their positions of influence in universities and on government committees to claim scientific status for their personal beliefs. Some of Cyril Burt's cursory assessments of parents' and indeed children's intelligence merely provide the best-known and most notorious examples.

Once a special facility is established, whether it be a subnormality hospital or a special school, power is vested in the people who control admissions to it. In the nineteenth century doctors claimed expertise in identifying 'patients' for subnormality institutions. They retained this power until after the 1944 Education Act, but were increasingly challenged by the new and rapidly developing profession of educational psychologists. Psychologists argued (a) that they had greater expertise in the 'scientific' assessment of intelligence, and (b) that, in any case, *educational* decisions could not sensibly be made on the basis of *medical* assessment. From 1975 LEAs were advised to consult educational psychologists before providing a special school place (DES, 1975). The 1981 Education Act required them to do so as part of the assessment leading to a formal statement of a child's special needs.

Yet all of this was predicated on the deficit model. In other words, assessment focused on what children could *not* do, and how they *differed* from other children. The Fish Report emphasised that the aims of education for children with special needs were the same as for all children (ILEA, 1985). Hence, an equally legitimate focus would be on what they *could* do, and on what they had in common with other children. This does not mean that we ignore a child's difficulties and the resources needed to overcome or reduce them. It does, nevertheless, imply that assessment of special educational needs leads in a different direction. The deficit model is orientated towards separate provision, either in a special school or by means of a withdrawal group for extra help with, say, reading. In contrast, the alternative model is orientated towards the 'normal' environment and the resources needed to enable this environment to cater adequately for the child.

Even this, however, can be criticised as having too narrow a focus on the individual child. Hargreaves (1982) has attacked the 'cult of individualism' which pervades education in Britain. Educational psychology has provided powerful support for this cult. The 1981 Education Act effectively created two categories of children with special needs: (a) those whose needs could be met within the school's existing resources, and *would not* need a formal assessment leading to the 'protection' of a statement of their special needs; (b) those whose needs could not be met without extra help, and who therefore *would* require a statement.

The problem here is that the need for extra help depends on the quality of resources currently available. Principal among these is the teacher. It follows that *children's* learning and behavioural difficulties may reveal their *teacher's* needs. The teacher may simply need additional resources, but the problem may also lie in teaching methods, classroom organisation, lesson preparation and the use of existing resources. In other words the needs of children and of teachers are interrelated.

All this can create substantial tensions for educational psychologists. Their only statutory responsibility is for assessment of special educational needs under the 1981 Education Act. In principle, the fact that they work in schools and with teachers enables them to see children's needs in the context of their school and classroom experience. In principle, then, educational psychologists are well placed to identify teachers' needs as well as children's, since in practice they are inextricably interrelated. In practice, visiting psychologists have to exercise the greatest caution to avoid appearing to 'blame' a teacher for a child's difficulties. To appear to be criticising a teacher colleague is to run the charge of being regarded as insensitive, ill-informed, even 'unprofessional'. In consequence, psychologists can often find themselves forced back on to a deficit model of special educational needs, seeing the problem as lying 'in' the child and/or the family.

Contrary, perhaps, to the intentions of legislation, the 1981 Education Act encouraged this tendency with its detailed requirements for formal assessment of special needs. These required LEAs to seek advice from teachers, an educational psychologist and a school doctor, and attempted to safeguard parents' interests by giving them numerous rights of consultation and of appeal against LEA decisions. Tutt (1985) has criticised the concept of special need implied in the Act as inappropriate, inadequate and detrimental. It is, he claims, inappropriate to children's interests in its focus on the individual child, with a corresponding neglect of the possible limitations in the school or classroom context; it is inadequate as it provides no guidance on the range or scope of special needs, nor on how or where they should be met. It is detrimental to children's interests by extending almost indefinitely the 'net' of children covered by a formal control system.

The first of Tutt's objections has created pressures on educational psychologists in some LEAs to define children's needs in the light of available resources (Goacher *et al.*, 1988). The reason, of course, lies in reluctance to accept expensive commitments at a time of financial restraint. LEAs have also varied widely in their policy on carrying out formal assessments. Few LEAs resist requests from parents, but they vary widely in how far they encourage their own teacher and educational psychologist employees to refer children for assessment. Some LEAs provide a statement for twice as many children as others (Goacher *et al.*, 1988).

The minutiae of assessment procedures may have had an additional consequence. The House of Commons (1987) Education, Science and Arts Committee received evidence from HMI, that few LEAs had adopted a coherent policy for special educational needs, and even fewer had formulated a coherent plan for implementing the policy they had adopted. The implication here is that the Act may have encouraged LEAs to respond to special needs as they arose in an *ad hoc* basis, without giving serious thought to the rationale for their overall provision or to its coherence. This led to some odd situations in which LEAs had formally adopted policies of integration, but continued to allocate resources in a way that made integration difficult, if not impossible to achieve (see Galloway and Goodwin, 1987; Galloway, 1990b).

The 1981 Education Act has nevertheless had some beneficial consequences. It has undoubtedly raised teachers' general awareness of the range and scope of children's learning and behavioural difficulties. It is also leading to more active parental participation in their children's assessment. Following from this, parents are becoming increasingly vocal and explicit in demanding the sort of provision they consider necessary. Often, though by no means invariably, this is in mainstream schools.

We are advocating a model that emphasises what children with special needs have in common with other children rather than their differences. This implies the importance for children with special needs, and for other children, of developing an appreciation of individual differences. In addition, the emphasis on the school and classroom context implicitly acknowledges the mutual adaptation that takes place between individuals and their social 'niche' (see Chapter 1). Recognising the scope and range of special educational needs and seeking to meet them in mainstream schools does not just have implications for the 2 per cent who had traditionally been taught in special schools, nor just for the 20, 40 or 50 per cent who were thought by Warnock, Sir Keith Joseph or HMI to have special needs, to be under-achieving or to have learning difficulties. It also has implications for all other pupils and for their teachers.

Conclusions

Teachers often perceive children with learning and behavioural problems as a source of stress. These children illustrate the limits to teachers' competence and threaten the stability of the classroom. The children concerned are disproportionately boys, from working-class families and members of ethnic minority groups. The evidence that at least 20 per cent of pupils have special needs at some stage in their school career, or according to HMI in Scotland 50 per cent, raises huge questions about the nature of the school system and its success in catering for large minorities of children.

Finding effective ways to teach children with a wide variety of abilities and backgrounds is part of each teacher's professional development. Relationships with children and seeing children making progress have been identified as the principal sources of job satisfaction for teachers (e.g. Holdaway, 1978 Galloway *et al.,* 1985). Seen in this light, children with special needs provide unique opportunities for job satisfaction The focus, though, will be on the quality of teaching for the class as a whole and on ways of meeting individual needs within the mainstream curriculum.

We can look at the similarities and differences between children in terms of their curricular entitlement and in terms of the teaching methods appropriate to their needs. The principles of metacognition and self-assessment apply as much in teaching children with special needs as in everything else teachers do in school. However, special needs impose particular pressures on teachers to recognise contextual influences on children's development. These naturally include the home environment. They also include the other children in the class, school and classroom organisation, the range, availability and use of resources, and teaching methods. In other words, effectiveness in identifying and catering for special needs is inextricably linked with the effectiveness in teaching the class as a whole. This, then, is an appropriate time to consider some recent work on classroom interaction.

Notes and further reading

1. The issues raised in this paragraph have been developed in work on the sociology and politics of special educational needs. See, for example, Barton (1988) and (1989) and Barton and Tomlinson (1984).
2. For further discussion of the 1981 Education Act, see: Hegarty (1987) and Dessent (1987).
3. Initial response to the 1988 Education Reform Act from special education were almost uniformly hostile. For an alternative perspective, which argues that the Act could have beneficial effects, see Galloway (1990c). In addition the National Curriculum Council appears to be taking an optimistic view, see NCC (1989a).

4. For a discussion of social learning theory, see Bandura (1974) and Bower and Hildegard (1981).
5. Recent books on a whole school approach to special educational needs have been written by Ainscow and Florek (1989) and Ramasut (1989).
6. For a more detailed account of the 'social control' perspective on special education, see Tomlinson (1982) and Thomas (1982).

Seminar suggestions

1. (a) Think of a child with special needs in the class you know best. Write 5–10 lines explaining why you regard this child as having special needs.
    (b) Now write a brief report of two or three paragraphs indicating the things this child *can* do, and how your future teaching with this child could build on the child's capabilities.
    In pairs discuss the different 'pictures' of each child that emerge from these two exercises. How far does the first lead to the deficit model described in the text, and the second to a whole school/class approach?
2. Describe the organisation of provision for special educational needs in the school each group member knows best. What are its strengths and limitations?
3. What methods do teachers in your school(s) use in assessing children's special educational needs? How far do these methods help teachers in planning future work with children? What alternatives are possible?

CHAPTER 4

Interaction in classrooms

Learning how to behave

From one perspective the transfer from primary to secondary schooling may involve children in abandoning the child-centred primary school culture and entering a knowledge-centred secondary school culture. This analysis quickly collapses under scrutiny as primary schools are becoming increasingly subject centred as a result of the National Curriculum and the introduction of management structures that are based on the coordination of subject expertise. At the same time secondary schools are moving into student-centred practices through the extension of TVEI-supported teaching methods, which include active learning and supported self-study across the curriculum.[1]

Yet the transition into secondary school is, as we have already indicated, a major rite of passage, and is frequently disturbing. One reason may be that transfer at eleven occurs a little too early for some children, prior to the onset of puberty and entry into adolescence. This dislocation of these two transitions may explain the *fussiness, anxiety* and *over-concern* of many primary school children as they move on into the next phase of schooling.

Most secondary schools are now addressing transfer problems by appointing primary link tutors who work with feeder schools and organise open events for incoming pupils. The work of Hamblin (1978) has been particularly influential here. However, pupil anxiety still exists and is kept under control in the settling down period by unnaturally formal behaviour which most frequently marks the first weeks of secondary schooling.

While teacher-organised transfer and link programmes can help to de-mystify uniforms, homework, school meals and similar points of information they do little to tackle what Measor and Woods (1984) call the informal concerns of incoming pupils. These centre on 'myths' which are relayed by preceding intakes; as we have already noted the famous example is 'head in a flushing toilet'. Measor and Woods suggest that these pupil myths demonstrate new demands to be made on pupils' endurance and character, and challenge a pupil's ability to adapt to these changes. In other words, the pupils are about to find themselves in a new situation to which they will have to adapt. Clarifying the demands of the formal elements of that situation is helpful, but gaps in knowledge about the informal aspects of being a secondary school pupil are filled by the acceptance of stories, which, though usually only half believed, serve the function of bridging the gap between primary and secondary school and providing a focus for pupil anxiety.

One major cause of that anxiety centres on the need to create a new identity in a new setting.[2] When this is coupled with the uncertainties and insecurities of pre-puberty the result is the fussiness that is so often a feature of first-year classrooms. Another related concern is loss of status and a resultant need to maintain self-esteem. This sometimes manifests itself as early 'deviancy' – for example, in the adaptation of uniform or pencil cases to reflect images of pre-teen popular culture.

Pupils carrying these concerns are met on their first day by teachers burdened with their own priorities. 'Keeping order' has to be central and the first few teacher–pupil encounters usually demonstrate that pupils are inducted out of junior school behaviour patterns into those of their new classrooms. While some rules are explicit (walk on the left hand side of the corridor) others are less so, but rely on teachers' cueing. Among other things pupils are encouraged to remain in their seats by teachers who mark work at pupils' desks and who discourage queuing. Measor and Woods (1984) give an interesting account of this induction process. Teachers therefore endeavour to ensure that pupils recognise their authority and ability to exert control. This occurs at the same time as the need for pupils gently to negotiate their way into their new identities. A dilemma is immediately established between the need for control and the need to establish relationships with the new intake of pupils. Finding the right balance presents particular problems to form tutors.

The first few weeks of secondary schooling are usually marked by excessive formality in behaviour and dress and by pupils fussing and demanding clarification; but as the negotiation process gets under way children learn what may and may not be done and start to work out their individual roles as pupils.

The pressures on teachers can be equally demanding as they too have to demonstrate to pupils the roles they have already created with previous intakes. It is less easy for them to adapt as their roles already exist and have in part been created by the demands of the job.

Classroom contexts

At first glance it would appear that the teacher as the creator of the contexts is very much in control of them. However, a closer look at selection of resources, planning of the classroom and choice of teaching styles reveals that teachers are, at least, guided by a variety of influences. Each department will have its curriculum priorities whether these are determined by government, school catchment area, locality, arbitrary decisions of the head or joint processes in staff meetings. These in turn are affected by the funding that represents national and local priorities. Resourcing is limited by finance and availability. Teaching styles and classroom organisation depend greatly on their acceptability to colleagues and Local Authority Inspectors. A hidden curriculum may be transmitted by the teacher but she or he is usually the agent of the value systems at work in the school if not the wider community. Teachers also respond to parental expectations if only to achieve a compromise. The learning contexts inhabited by pupils, then, appear to be constructed by teachers who represent prevailing cultural and political priorities.

These contexts also require different behaviours. Music lessons may demand creativity and collaboration, science may require collaboration but creativity has to be curbed. Some English teachers encourage discussion, while others are wary of it. As pupils move on through the school new learning styles are encouraged through TVEI- related programmes. Pupils may be expected to undertake supported self-study in History but not in Geography. Craft subjects allow an informal relationship as the teacher works alongside the pupil, while more academic subjects may discourage this. Pupils learn to read the cues on how far they can go, but add to this reading their own evaluations of the status of the subject. Worthwhile subjects are less likely to be undermined.

As interactions not only occur in contexts, but are to an extent determined by them, it is important that any examination of classroom interactions take situations into account. This point is not only of relevance to understanding the notion of classroom interaction at a theoretical level, but also to the daily assessments that teachers make of pupils. If it is evident that a learner has problems with one teacher or in one subject, then enquiry has to start from there.

Becoming a pupil

At the more theoretical level, what we have been arguing is that 'being a secondary school pupil' is a 'niche' which is waiting to be occupied and into which the young person enters. Shotter (1984), as seen in Chapter 1, has described childhood in much these terms. He talks of the opportunities for development available to children as the niche that their culture has created for them in order to turn them into the adults that culture desires. The experiences or opportunities for development available within secondary schools are constructed with the intention of shaping young people into effective learners and manageable members of the learning group. When these intentions are not realised we need to look at the developmental opportunities as they exist within the niche as well as at the pupil. Paul Willis's (1977) work on the responses to schooling of adolescent male non-academic pupils gives a clear example of how roles are negotiated within the constraints of available opportunities. In the case of Willis's young men the response was to create a counter-culture within which they could successfully and effectively operate.

It follows, then, that when we talk of interaction we cannot regard it as a one-way process. While the young person adapts to becoming a pupil of a specific school, elements of the classroom or school niche are also accommodating to the pupil's demands. Thus teachers may rearrange timetables, or use new techniques or resources to achieve their ends. The child as pupil is produced as a result of negotiations between the child as learner and the teachers who create a specific pupil niche. Pupils have to renegotiate with each adult as they move around the school. They soon become adept at this as usually expectations of their behaviour fall into a clear range and teacher cues are remarkably similar (French and Peskett, 1986).

Shotter (1984) described the aim of childhood as the creation of autonomous adults: while this may be true of many cultures, there may be more debate over whether it is the aim of schooling. Developmental psychologists (e.g. Newson, 1974; Schaffer, 1977; Trevarthen, 1977) argue that children learn to become autonomous, free-standing members of society as a result of high-quality interactions with their early carers. High-quality interactions involve the adult in 'turn taking', mutual respect and tuning in to the world of the child. So important is mutuality that in the very early stages the adult acts as if there is equality in the relationship, even though the infant cannot yet participate, and subsequently the child is encouraged to enter the dialogue as a full partner as soon as possible.

Can it be said that dialogues of this quality regularly occur in classrooms? Habermas (1972) talks of true communication as best achieved between equal partners in a dialogue. The world of the school and demands made on teachers would seem to make this unlikely. It is difficult to find examples in everyday adult life which might illustrate the sense of powerlessness experienced by some pupils in classrooms. This may be particularly the case in secondary schools where the day for teachers and pupils is dominated by timetable demands and rules over which there can be no negotiation.

Language and learning

Yet clearly the quality of social interaction is now regarded as an important element in good teaching. While still maintaining the belief that children need to construct their own understanding of events, effective practitioners recognise the importance of language to the learner's cognitive processes. The work of Bruner and Vygotsky in this field will be discussed in Chapter 5 when we examine cognition and teaching. Their influence is certainly evident in the current emphasis on what Walkerdine and Sinha (1978) describe as 'discourse formats', for example in science and mathematics.

Working with children of secondary school age, Assessment of Performance Unit teams examining children's performance in science and language tasks found direct links between levels of performance, with use of language a crucial aspect. They argue that:

...the view of 'language structure' as something wider and more coherent than word or single concepts is coming to be recognised as increasingly important to the way children cope with or fail to meet the demands of different school subjects. (White, 1988, p. 5)

Making a similar point, the Cockcroft Report states: 'Language plays an essential part in the formation and expression of mathematical ideas' (DES, 1982, para. 306).

Language specialists also emphasise language use and the matching of discourse to context. Talking in terms of assessment, the Kingman Committee (DES, 1988c, p. 57) stated:

We recognise ... the notion that crucial features of language use relate to the specific situation and the precise task undertaken whatever the subject and that one cannot infer that a different task will produce the same kind of response.

Children have to master considerable complexities of language use. It would appear that interaction with adults is an essential part of this process. If pupils are to learn, i.e. construct meaning in interaction with adults, the quality of that interaction is all important. Pupils need to use language appropriately and teachers need to see them do so. This exercise calls for the kind of relationship that Habermas was suggesting when he indicated that the ideal interaction was based on mutual respect and trust.

Talking with children

Nowhere is the need for these qualities more evident than in the diagnostic setting. This kind of information can only be elicited if it is to be received in a non-judgemental fashion with genuine interest, in order to be used as a starting point for further teaching. However, the all pervasive power imbalance resulting from the teachers' need for authority and control so easily militates against what we might want to call 'real conversation'.

In order to discover how children are making sense of a subject teachers need to establish an atmosphere or climate in which the learners can put forward their own explanations of events or topics. It is only when pupils feel free enough to offer their interpretations that teachers have ready access to what learners are thinking. Part of the process of learning is to do with discarding, often quite firmly held, 'alternative constructions' of the subject-matter in order to start to approximate the agreed constructions held by subject experts. We shall see in Chapter 5 how teachers can help learners to shift from alternative (or inaccurate) ways of understanding to those more commonly held. The job of teachers is made a little easier if they can begin to understand the misconceptions held by pupils and so plan routes for pupil learning. Learners are much more likely to make their misconceptions explicit in relatively relaxed task-orientated conversations. This claim is made evident in research studies in science education (Driver, 1983) and in the work of the Secondary Science Curriculum Review team (SSCR, 1983).

The importance of the quality elements of conversation is particularly evident in studies of the relative frequency of teacher and pupil questions. Wood (1988) reports two studies, one of British pre-school children and the other of American high school students. In these studies the frequency of teacher questions as a percentage of all utterances was 47 per cent in the British study and 43 per cent in the American investigation. By contrast, children's questions accounted for 4 per cent and 8 per cent of utterances, respectively. Indeed, teacher questions seemed to inhibit child talk; the more frequently the teacher asked questions, the less the pupils talked about the topic, asked questions or talked to each other. It seemed that teachers were controlling through questioning and not permitting authentic dialogues.

Yet teachers appear to value the use of questions to encourage children's thinking and understanding. Brown and Edmondson (1984) found that this was the most frequently given reason for questions by their sample of teachers of 11 to 13 year-olds. The most commonly used types of questions were selected to elicit simple deductions or comparisons and to encourage recall, for example, of procedures or knowledge. Both categories of questions would tend to arise in situations where the child would feel that the teacher was expecting the right answer. Clearly the skills of diagnosis call for subtlety and a conducive classroom ethos.

Negotiating for control

An attempt to analyse classroom life to enable the examination of interactions in different contexts has been carried out by Doyle (1983, 1986) in the United States. Taking the idea of negotiation between teacher and pupil as central to the avoidance of chaos in classrooms, he has provided a useful framework for understanding classroom interactions. This will be elaborated in terms of children's learning and classroom management in Chapters 5 and 6. The teacher's concern, he argues, is to maintain order so that learning can occur. At the same time the pupil's concern is to avoid taking risks so that teacher approval is likely. Doyle observes that tasks which call for high-level cognitive processes such as reasoning or problem solving tend to appear ambiguous to pupils who, in turn, try to avoid risk by demanding more detailed explanation and guidance. If teachers do not respond, pupil disruption may occur with the result that teachers may decide to eliminate these high-risk tasks at the outset.

Doyle's analysis is useful because it allows us to see classroom life as a process of negotiation in which both participant groups, pupils and teachers, are to an extent vulnerable. From this perspective we cannot really understand classroom interaction unless we see the teacher's need to control as clearly as the child's need to please. In the 1986 review he proposes that both under- and over-control on the part of the teacher is non-conducive to challenging children into thinking, and advocates an intermediate level in which teachers and pupils interact frequently to sustain order so that potential disorder is eradicated before it matures. He therefore sees effective pupil teacher interaction as crucial to creating the learning environment. This belief is supported in a British study by French and Peskett (1986). They pointed out that any worthwhile interaction between pupils and teacher 'presupposes' order and attention. Teachers, therefore, have a fine balancing act to sustain when undertaking diagnostic questioning. At one level they need to demonstrate the respect they have for children's construction of experiences in order to base their teaching on the pupil's current level of understanding. At another level they need to maintain the order necessary for an effective learning environment. In the continuous process of negotiation that appears to occur in classrooms they have to be seen to be successful. If diagnostic questioning demands that children become more equal partners in negotiations across all aspects of classroom life, then teachers may feel that they are taking risks. Doyle suggests that tensions of this type are resolved through an increased emphasis on general classroom management. By setting up durable well-defined work systems for pupils, teachers establish a substructure of order against which negotiations are enacted. In effect, warm and democratic classroom climates that are conducive to effective learning depend upon carefully designed and controlled infrastructures of appropriate pupil tasks. The effective setting of these tasks, in turn, depends upon accurate diagnosis of pupils' starting points for learning. These points will be elaborated in Chapter 6.

Pupil–pupil interaction

Interactions with teachers may be problematic for pupils but pupils also interact with each other. This interaction may not always be to their academic advantage. Wheldall *et al.* (1981) compared the on-task behaviour of 11-year-old children when seated in rows and at tables and found that time on task was greater when the children were seated in rows facing the teacher. Wheldall (1985) pre-empts any simplistic interpretations of these data, suggesting that tables may prove more suitable for topic work or small group discussions. A similar study by Bennett and Blundell (1983) found that the quantity of children's work increased while they were seated in rows while the quality remained constant across rows and tables.

These studies may well tell us more about the way in which group work has been perceived in primary classrooms since the Plowden Report (CACE, 1967) than about the potential offered by this method of managing pupil learning. Bennett (1985a) summarises the state of group work in primary schools when he states that 'pupils work *in* groups but not *as* groups'.

Grouping as an organisational strategy has not always lent itself easily to secondary schooling. This has not simply been due to an emphasis on delivery of knowledge in post-11 schooling, as other related constraints have militated against wider development of these methods. Of these timetabling and the multi-purpose use of classrooms have provided the severest obstacles. Nevertheless, demands made by the GCSE for group presentations and the development of oracy together with a concern with personal and social education, often supported by TVEI initiatives, have meant that group work is certainly an important feature in the school day of older secondary school pupils.

An important element in the rationale for interactive group work is that it provides situations in which pupils can test and try ideas and therefore start to engage in processes of evaluating their own work. Encouraging pupil self-evaluation may well necessitate careful groundwork by the teacher as pupils are frequently set into behaviour patterns focused on producing end products to satisfy teachers' demands.

Yeomans (1983), in a research report on collaborative group work in primary and secondary schools, implies that the initial effort might be worth while. A feature of the American research, she notes, is that collaborative group work is particularly effective when attempting tasks demanding high-level cognitive processes, i.e. greater risks in Doyle's (1983) terms. Personal and social development also appear to be enhanced. Mutual concern develops, relationships across racial background are improved and positive feelings towards school are increased. The work of Barnes (1976) would also suggest that this is true of English pupils. Yeomans does, however, observe that there is limited empirical evidence to support these claims. This qualification is also raised by Bennett who suggests that the field of group processes and learning has much to offer researchers (Bennett, 1985a). It may be timely for social and cognitive psychologists to collaborate in interactive cooperative research groups.³

To return to the control issue raised by Doyle's work (Doyle, 1986), collaborative group work does take immediate control of events away from the teacher and calls for a form of interaction between pupil and teacher in which the teaching emphasis is on process rather than product and where judgements on process are made by the collaborating pupils as they constantly evaluate and adapt their responses to the task. Responsibility for the evaluation of process and outcome is clearly an element to be considered when pupil–teacher interaction occurs. As Edwards (1988) has argued, when teachers recognise pupils' rights to self-evaluation the possibility of an interaction that may truly inform teachers about pupils' learning is more likely. Barnes (1976) and Barnes and Todd (1977) have examined the relationship between curriculum quality and classroom interactions and suggest that an emphasis on high quality interactions, focused on the processes of learning which is underpinned by a willingness of teachers to regard classroom communication as two way, is beneficial to pupil learning, and the use of collaborative group work is one way to achieve this end.

Teachers' perception of children

If two-way communication in classrooms is to be effective in optimising pupil learning, teachers have to endeavour to enter that communication willing to seek and understand the frameworks used by children to organise their experience. No communication is ever perfect, as everyone brings their own experiences and nuances of meanings to interactions, and teachers dealing with large numbers of pupils are bound to draw on their experiences to create quick and reliable frameworks or stereotypes to enable them to organise their interactions with pupils and so render the situations more predictable.

Kelly's theory of personal constructs (Kelly, 1955; Bannister and Fransella, 1971) gives us a useful basis for examining the way our anticipations guide our behaviours. Arguing that we enter any interaction with expectations formed during previous experiences and with a set of limited and personal criteria against which we evaluate the other person, Kelly provides us with a way of understanding the constraints we place on others and ourselves.

Research into teacher attitudes to girls reveals a comparable state of affairs. Pratt (1985) reports the result of a survey of secondary school teacher attitudes to equal opportunities in school. The survey reveals that nearly half his sample of over 850 teachers appears to be unsympathetic towards equality of opportunity for pupils. Whyte (1983) argues that an even greater challenge faces primary schools. She points out that the comfortable world of the primary school, where the conformity of girls is expected and welcomed, only encourages girls to please adults and avoid the risk taking often necessary in learning. This analysis receives support in the work of Walden and Walkerdine (1985).

Similarly, as we have already indicated, Dweck's study of learned helplessness (Dweck *et al.*, 1978) reported that teachers accounted for the poor performances of girls in terms of 'intellectual inadequacies' while they attributed boys' low performances to poor motivation. That is, the girls were seen as innately incapable and unlikely to improve while the boys might be worth some perseverance to improve motivation and hence performance.

These issues are important because children learn about themselves in interaction with others. Teachers are a particularly powerful source of information about the self, or personal identity, for young children since they may be regarded as 'significant others' (Mead, 1934). Harré (1983) has usefully described personal identity as an important organising principle. In this sense children's actions are directed by their sense of self-efficacy which, in turn, may be determined by what the child feels she or he is allowed to do. To limit that sense by clinging to the constraints of stereotyping is to restrict the range of options of behaviour open to the child and so limit learning and development.

Tajfel (1978) makes some interesting comments on the phenomenon of the stereotype. He observes that the less information one holds about a person the more likely it is that group-related characteristics are assigned to that person. This may be relatively harmless if it is merely a way of flexibly classifying someone until more information is available. However, if there is an 'emotional charge', which may be fed by strong prejudices, then stereotypes tend to be rigid and not amenable to change.

Again the value of a real information-seeking dialogue in which children's perspectives are received non-judgementally would seem to be one way of recasting role stereotypes more flexibly. While emotionally charged rigid stereotypes may be hard to deal with, the role of the school in providing information and encouraging cross-cultural interaction to prevent the construction of such prejudices is evident.

The control dimension

It seems that it is impossible to get away from the tension that lies at the root of pupil–teacher interaction. Effective teachers recognise that equal and open communication with pupils is conducive to the accurate diagnosis of needs, which is essential to their planning of tasks. They are aware that tasks which entail cognitive challenge tend to involve risk taking and that this may lead to insecurity, fear of teacher judgement and avoidance strategies on the part of children. Equally they know that order and control over incipient chaos is a prerequisite to any teaching and learning and, as a result, they appear to place the control need over the communication need. As we stated earlier, interactions are in part determined by the contexts in which they occur. Control is clearly important as teachers have the day-to-day responsibility for the safety and general discipline of their pupils. In addition, they teach alongside colleagues who expect order. For most teachers a slip in the control of pupils is far more immediately evident than errors in curriculum planning.

It would be pessimistic to assume that these factors necessarily militate against good classroom interactions. A more positive step is to examine ways in which the quality of interaction may be improved within existing contexts.

Improving the quality of interaction

If we take the ideal model of teacher–pupil interaction to be one of mutual regard in which the learner feels assured that his or her contributions are valued, we need to examine teaching strategies that will permit the pupil to enter the dialogue armed with a sense of his or her own rights and responsibilities. This kind of interaction, as we have already argued, is impossible to achieve when the pupil feels that the teacher's prime concern is hearing the one correct answer. The processes of classroom interaction have to be consistent. Learners may find it difficult to take creative risks in problem-solving tasks when in a previous science session teacher evaluations of their responses had dominated. Several strategies need to be employed simultaneously to ensure the appropriate classroom ethos if the desired dialogue is to take place.

1. *The self-evaluating pupil*
Nisbet and Shucksmith (1986) start their examination of children's learning strategies with the assertion that learning how to learn is in fact the most important learning. Drawing on the notion of metacognition or an awareness of one's own mental process, they argue that to recognise and manage task demands is essential to successful learning. Usefully taking this idea to classroom practice they discuss learning strategies which they consider to be 'higher order skills' that monitor the use of the lower order practical skills demanded by the task. These strategies are outlined in more detail in Chapter 5.

Brown and De Loache (1983) make a similar claim for the importance of what they term metacognitive skills or behaviour for 'coordinating and controlling' learning. They emphasise the transferability of these skills across the child's learning experiences to the extent that they should be applied whenever a new task is met.

Both pairs of psychologists argue that these strategies should be taught in schools. Acquisition has the effect of freeing the child from the constant need to seek teacher approval. Once goals have been clearly established the child should be responsible for monitoring his or her progress towards those goals. There are, of course, implications for pupil–teacher interactions during that progress as the teacher has to stand back and allow pupil decision making to proceed.

2. Asking questions

Bruner (1974) has argued that children's questions reveal more about their understanding than do their answers. At another level, Nisbet and Shucksmith (1986) consider asking questions about the task to be an important learning strategy. Teachers' responses to children's questions provide the key to the quality of the interaction. Taking diagnosis as a starting point for teaching, it may be appropriate to respond with a question that explores the way the child is making sense. Those questions demanding further information, for example, 'what if...?' or 'what would happen next?', are useful. Equally, encouraging the process of learning how to learn may necessitate bouncing the question back to the child for the required evaluation – for example, 'What do you think?' To create an ethos in which true, undistorted communication can occur it is necessary to attend to the type and use of teacher questions and to allow some control to the child.

3. Valuing process

A prerequisite to the notion of 'independent learner' and a corollary of the recognition of the power of teacher questions is a need to emphasise the processes that lead to task completion in order to provide a counter-balance to a focus on the quality of the final outcome. Any task set by teachers may make a range of demands on learners. Bennett *et al.* (1984) provide a useful introduction to the complexities of task analysis. Equally, the strategies outlined by Nisbet and Shucksmith (1986) suggest it is possible to identify specific process skills that can be signalled to the child as important.

Once the 'how' as well as the 'what' of task completion is seen to be valued the child is, to an extent, freed from problems of the finality of teacher judgements of outcomes and able to operate in a situation where teacher help with process skills may be requested without fear of failing to please.

4. *The self-evaluating teacher*

The suggestions made in this chapter for improving interaction in classrooms require considerable teacher self-awareness. To ensure that teacher questions are appropriate, that children are using their learning strategies independently or working effectively in groups, demands constant monitoring of classroom processes. Simple strategies such as tape recording oneself leading a class discussion, or placing a cassette recorder on a table where two children are engaged in a problem-solving task will yield rich information on teaching styles and the contributions of pupils.

Effective teachers spend a lot of time listening to pupils. Within an interactionist model of pedagogy it is important that they are also aware of the cues, messages and opportunities that they present to pupils. The only way to achieve this is through careful monitoring of practice followed by self-reflection.

The aim of this activity is not to disempower or undermine the confidence of practitioners, though it can be a challenging experience. On the contrary, the self-evaluating teacher emerges from the experience strengthened by a greater understanding of his or her own pedagogy and with fresh insights into ways in which it might be developed. Stressing, as we do in this volume, the importance of the teacher to children's learning we are bound to emphasise the need for teachers to be alert to all elements of their own practice.

Notes and further reading

1. The Technical and Vocational Education Initiative (TVEI) had a considerable impact on secondary schools in the 1980s. Of particular relevance to issues raised in this book are two volumes in the TVEI 'Developments' series: Developments 5, *Profiles and Records of Achievement* and Developments 10, *Flexible Learning,* published by the Training Agency, Moorfoot, Sheffield, S1 4PQ. More information on TVEI and literature produced as a result of the initiative can be provided by TVEI A(3), 236 Grays Inn Road, London, WC1X 8HL (addresses correct at time of going to press).

2. For a good introduction to social identity and the construction of identity, see Pervin (1984). For more challenging reading on this topic see Harré (1979) and (1983) and Shotter (1984).

3. The issues of power and control in educational settings are well documented in the field of sociology of education – see, for example, Apple, (1979) and (1983), Barton and Meighan (1978) and Whitty and Young (1976).

Seminar suggestions

1. Ask students to tape record themselves introducing a new 'object', e.g. a piece of equipment or a stimulus for discussion to two children: a boy and a girl. A few minutes of the recording should be transcribed and

brought to the seminar. Extracts can be discussed in pairs or by the whole group to explore the distribution of power in interaction, how it was exercised and controlled and the implications for the student's own model of how children best learn.

This recording can be used for similar exercises to explore ideas raised in Chapters 5 and 6.

2. Ask students to distinguish the rules and rituals of the seminar. What are their purposes? How are they played? How are they learned? How might the seminar be done better? What are the time implications for classroom teaching? Why do teachers work in the way they do? How might it be done better?

CHAPTER 5

How do learners make sense of the information around them?

Making sense of school

Schools are hectic, busy places and pupils work hard to impose some shape or form on their experiences there. We have already indicated that these efforts can result either in conformity to rules or in the creation of counter-cultures which enable pupils clearly to place their own frames of reference on school events. Similarly, the amount of information and the range of skills to be passed on to pupils can be bewildering.

As pupils move around the school in routines that are dominated by timetabling and room allocation rather than by the individual pupils, they are faced with arrays of information, skills to learn and stimuli to respond to. They need direction if they are to use limited subject time effectively. In this situation the major function of the teacher is to ensure that pupils pay attention to those aspects of classroom life which offer optimal learning experiences.

Doyle (1986) has described classrooms as confusing places in which both pupils and teachers negotiate order out of incipient chaos and in which teachers help pupils to place order on their learning experience by aiding them in making appropriate selections from the stimuli competing for attention. During the course of this chapter we shall suggest that the teacher's role extends beyond this, as Doyle (1983) has argued, to involve a sophisticated understanding of children and of the tasks provided by teachers. This claim is no more than an attempt to clarify the relationship between theories of how pupils learn and what is sometimes elusively labelled good practice.

By the time children enter secondary school they have already experienced at least seven years of the institutionalised citizen-creating process we call schooling.

From whatever political perspective we view education systems, there would be little dispute over that statement (Apple, 1985; Walkerdine, 1984). Pupils are expected to acquire the skills, concepts and attitudes of the prevailing culture. The implementation of a National Curriculum is current testament to that. There is nothing unusual in this expectation of education. Cole (1985) is one of many psychologists who take a cross-cultural perspective to demonstrate how, even in relatively primitive societies, the role of the adult is to instruct the child into ways of maintaining existing cultural competencies and priorities.

However, teaching in school is probably more problematic than, for example, the apprenticeship situation among the Zinacantecan weavers of Mexico described by Cole. Teaching has evolved into a professional occupation which involves engagement with the processes of pedagogy. Although it may be difficult to describe a commonly held and articulated model of pedagogy, it is likely that there would be some agreement on the need for the pupil to become an effective and independent learner. That this statement may, in fact, be based on a range of assumptions about teaching and learning and hence used to support a variety of forms of pedagogy will be evident in the course of this chapter. This ambivalence is of little help to the teaching profession at a time when the lack of a coherent view of effective pedagogy has rendered it vulnerable to curriculum design backed by legislation. Psychology has either not always served the profession well (Donaldson, 1978; Walkerdine, 1984) or appears to have had little impact on teachers (Zeichner *et al.,* 1987). Nevertheless, our belief is that effective teaching can be underpinned by a clear model of children's learning and the importance of teachers to that model. Further, if teaching is to be regarded as more than a mechanistic exercise that model needs to be understood by teachers to the extent that it informs their day-to-day classroom decision making.

The Piagetian inheritance

The insights provided by Piaget's research into the ways that children make sense of their environment are considerable. His major contributions were: (a) to focus the attention of teachers on to the possibility that children at different stages of cognitive development were interpreting experiences in different ways from adults; and (b) to provide an explanatory model of the learning process which still holds water as one of the 'best bets' available.

While not dwelling either on the intricacies of each stage of development (see Table 5.1) or on the extensive critique of his work (Donaldson, 1978; Brown and Desforges, 1979), the notion of stages focused attention on the developing mental structures of the child and the importance of matching learning experiences to the child's ability to cope with them: this has been a crucially important stimulus to the development of current pedagogy. As we can see from Table 5.1, it has also provided a justification for the age structure of the British school system. (See Shayer and Adey (1981) for a useful critique of ages and stages.)

Table 5.1 **Piaget's stages of development**

I	The Sensori-Motor Period	(Infancy)
II	The Pre-operational Period	(Pre-school and infant school)
III	The Concrete Operative Period	(Junior schools)
IV	The Formal Operations Period	(Secondary schooling)

Similarly, the explanatory mechanisms Piaget provided to demonstrate the processes of learning have had far-reaching consequences for the practice of teaching. Understanding these processes necessitates getting to grips with the terms 'assimilation' and 'accommodation' (see Table 5.2)

Table 5.2 **Piaget's intellectual processes**

Assimilation
The organism (mind) deals with new events by making them fit into its existing structures. The organism does not adapt itself to the new information. This needs to be balanced by some form of:

Accommodation
The organism (mind) adapts to the new events, for example, new concepts are formed or existing ones extended to incorporate and make sense of the new information.

In addition to emphasising the importance of careful sequencing of experience to ensure accommodation, this model places the pupil actively at the centre of his or her own learning.

The prominence accorded Piaget's work enabled practitioners to see children as active learners who construct models of the world using the mental processes of which they are developmentally capable.

The effect on pedagogy has been to encourage adults to look at and listen to children and to consider the appropriateness of the learning experiences provided. Another equally important point explicit in Piaget's biological model of child development was a view of intelligence as intelligent behaviour, or appropriate adaptation to one's environment. His work was instrumental in making a case for the psychological foundations of pedagogy and has provided new generations of developmental and cognitive psychologists with a field of study in which psychological knowledge can have important practical applications.

Theories of child development and theories of instruction

... the heart of the educational process consists of providing aids and dialogues for translating experience into more powerful systems of notation and ordering. And it is for this reason that I think a theory of development must be linked to both a theory of knowledge and to a theory of instruction, or be doomed to triviality. (Bruner, 1966, p. 21)

The assumptions within this statement are profound and need to be addressed if pedagogy is to be regarded as something more than enhancing the 'natural' developmental processes of the pupil. First, we need to assume that what the teacher does may affect the success of the desired learning and, secondly, that what is to be learned needs to be understood by the adult to the extent that he or she is able to order and organise the experiences of information to be tackled by the child.

The belated translation of Vygotsky's work into English (e.g. Vygotsky, 1962 and 1978) has provided educationalists with an alternative to Piagetian theory. Whereas the Piagetian model of children's thinking would explain a child's inability to handle new information or tasks simply as lack of maturity in their intellectual structures, the framework supplied by Vygotskian theory would allow us to see the failure to cope both in developmental terms and in terms of a lack of relevant prior experiences, with a consequent inability to make appropriate connections to existing knowledge. The fundamental difference between the two views is that while Piagetian theory allows educationalists to talk of the 'natural' development of the child's cognitive structures, the Vygotskian perspective places the 'teacher' firmly alongside the child in a process of jointly constructing meaning and so emphasises the importance of language and communication in the construction of an understanding of the world.[1]

Very young children learn from their adult care-givers who take pains to emphasise those aspects of the child's experience they believe to be of importance. In this way children are inducted into their culture and are able to begin to take on the accumulated knowledge which constitutes that culture. Adult highlighting of significant events and experiences occurs through dialogue and other forms of interaction (Newson, 1977). When we see school learning as part of that process of induction into a culture, begging the question, of course, of which culture, we can learn a lot from the strategies used by care-givers in infancy and early childhood.

At the centre of this interactive view of learning is the notion of infant and child intentionality, as conversations or interactions imply some intentionality on both sides. In the first few years of life healthy development includes an enhanced sense of the ability effectively to set and attain personal goals. Over-dependency on the care-giver can impede the ability to take responsibility for setting goals and taking action.

Parallels may be drawn here with flexible learning strategies – for example, supported self-study (Waterhouse, 1988) – which demand some student goal setting and evaluation of performance. Interactive models of learning also place the teacher in a position in which in varying ways he or she may make a direct impact on the learning process.

Learning a culture involves adopting the categorisations of the culture in which we grow up. The role of the adult in this view of learning is to bring the child to the categorisation processes that are commonly used. The role of the teacher is to select from the culture those skills or concepts which the child both needs and has the experience necessary to acquire.

Bruner again summarises this process when he describes mental growth as something

dependent upon growth from the outside in, a mastery of techniques that are embodied in the culture and that are passed on in a contingent dialogue by agents of the culture (Bruner, 1966, p. 21).

How does the learner make sense?

So far we have indicated the importance of the adult to children's learning and have suggested that pupils are actively engaged in a process of constructing meaning or categorising the information they perceive. Humans try to make sense of new information by relating it to what they already know and by trying to fit it to their pre-existing information categories. If the information does not fit easily, the categories may need to be altered in order to accommodate the new information.

To shift categories or mental constructs can be difficult and even painful, as mental constructs are interrelated with the result that a change in the limits of one may necessitate a corresponding change in other related constructs. As might be expected this process becomes more difficult with age and experience as constructs eventually become embedded in complex systems of understanding. When these constructs do not accord with those recognised as appropriate by the culture, it is the job of the teacher to support learners as they shed or adjust their 'alternative constructs'. Clearly, helping learners to reconstruct events or experiences will depend on careful diagnosis of their current understanding; consequently the processes need to be supported by what Watts and Bentley (1987) describe as a 'non-threatening learning environment'. They argue that conceptual change demands a considerable degree of 'self-exposure' by the learner to enable diagnosis and that, as a result, relationships based on trust, sympathy and empathy between teacher and learner are crucial. This, they explain, can help bridge the gap between the high-status authority of teacher knowledge and the more tentative intuitive and unique understandings of individual learners. To learn successfully in school is to be able to move from personal alternative constructions to those currently accepted as correct or appropriate.

Another way of supporting this change is to systematically induct the child into the 'discourse' of the subject. We have already seen in Chapter 4 how pupils might be inducted into the discourse or rules of secondary schooling and so move quickly to becoming effective operators within the system. Similarly, we may argue that different subjects establish their own sets of rules, expectations and meanings which are ascribed to specific words. Consequently, an important aid to a pupil's categorisation of knowledge is access to the language and rules that operate on a subject.

Entry into a discourse can mean more than access to, for example, relevant symbol use. Language itself can be a powerful guide to thought. Vygotsky (1978) argues that language and thought work together in what he describes as a 'dialectical unity', so that each enhances the contribution of the other to achieving understanding. Wells, while writing about concept acquisition in young children, puts the same idea more clearly:

existing concepts provide a clue to the meanings of words heard, and words heard lead to a modification of existing concepts, with the situational context in both cases providing additional support in establishing the relationship on particular occasions. (Wells, 1981, p. 81)

He then proceeds to make the case for the overall importance of language, as once it is acquired it 'becomes a means of extending the range and complexity of thought' (p. 87). Linguistic representations appear to release pupils from the here and now to enable them to extrapolate, make connections and construct their own meaning systems.

It is evident, however, that different styles of language use impact differently on children's thinking. Phillips' (1985) study of pupil language in group work indicated that a range of linguistic strategies or styles operated, but that some were more conducive to pupils' thinking than were others. The lesson for teachers from Phillips' work is clear: to focus on language acquisition is not enough, learners need the opportunity to engage in language use which enables them to operate at more cognitively challenging levels. That this kind of talk tends to occur in structured pupil groups will be picked up again in Chapter 6.

The role of the adult

As we have already argued, the interplay between language and action in the construction of meaning certainly suggests that adult and learner need to work alongside each other for at least part of the learning process. Vygotsky (1978) has provided teachers with a useful model of teacher–pupil roles in this learning process. He suggests that when we make a judgement about a child's intellectual capacity we must examine two developmental levels. The first is the 'actual developmental level' of the learner and is assessed on what the pupil can do now as a result of previous learning. The second level, the level of potential development, is assessed on the basis of what the learner is able to do after careful teaching. Vygotsky argued that indications of the pupil's ability to learn from others were more revealing than a measure based upon the previous learning achieved, as the latter might simply reflect the developmental opportunities available. The difference between the actual developmental level and the level of potential development he termed the zone of proximal development (ZPD). The ZPD is more than a diagnostic model. Vygotsky saw it in pedagogical terms, as developmental processes internal to the child are triggered to come into operation when he or she interacts with the adults who mediate or pass on the culture. As a consequence the pupil's learning has to be structured by careful selection and organisation of information and experiences. Vygotsky's emphasis on the role of the teacher is explicit, as it is usually the interaction with adults which sets off internal changes in the young learner's mental construction of the world. The adult's role may be to introduce new ideas and information and then to provide the learner with further opportunities to consolidate that new information and to make the necessary adjustments in his or her existing system of mental constructs. A typical sequence would be for the teacher to interact with the learner in the initial stages of taking on new skills or information in order to model the skills or use appropriate language, and then to encourage the learner to incorporate these new elements into his or her own actions through carefully planned task setting. These are the processes that are described by Wood (1988) as the scaffolding provided by teachers.

Matching task and pupil

The description of the pedagogic processes described by Vygotsky points to the degree of responsibility that the teacher holds for the child's learning. He writes: 'properly organised learning results in mental development and sets in motion a variety of developmental processes that would be impossible apart from learning' (Vygotsky, 1978, p. 90).

It is the 'proper organisation' of the learning that is the key. This implies careful diagnostic assessment of the learner's existing category system and appropriate sequencing of learning experiences to enable the learner to move from that point towards the next defined curricular goal. Ausubel put it another way when he admonished teachers to find out 'where the child is at, and teach him accordingly' (Ausubel, 1968).

Matching the task to the pupil at the very least therefore involves assessment of the learner's existing ways of understanding events and his or her ability to deal with the new information, together with a fine analysis of the relevant curriculum in order to enable careful and appropriate sequencing of information or skills. The latter is as important as the former. Driver (1983) argues that teachers have to regard children's inadequate categorisation of scientific knowledge as 'alternative frameworks' and that they have to take these as their starting points with pupils while endeavouring to ensure that there is little opportunity for proliferation of such frameworks as they only provide obstacles to effective learning. Pointing out the improbability that pupils will 'discover' the models and conventions of current scientific thought, she proposes that a clear role for the teacher is to 'help children assimilate their practical experiences into what is possibly a new way of thinking about them' (Driver, 1983, p. 9).

Driver's work illustrates the two major aspects of match: the need to understand the learner and the need to know the sequence of skills and concepts relevant to a particular curriculum area. The work of Norman (1978) and a subsequent study by Bennett *et al.* (1984) suggest that the two-dimensional framework so far outlined is simply a starting point. Norman starts with the premise already proposed: that new information interacts with the learning in existing organised mental structures. Successful learning occurs when that new input is integrated with appropriate existing categories. He isolated three processes at work in the experience of learning: accretion, restructuring and tuning. Accretion is the first phase and may involve the child in the initial acquisition of facts or the introduction to skills. During the second phase, the existing category system is restructured to accommodate the new information and old information is provided with new insights from fresh input. During the final phase of learning, new skills and ways of understanding are fine tuned or practised until they appear to be used 'automatically'. All three phases are essential to successful learning and although they may not be separated out into clearly distinct sequential phases, their relative importance to the process of learning is in the sequence of accretion, restructuring and tuning just described.

This analysis of potential task demand can be of enormous help to teachers in the management of teaching time; for example, the need for teacher input or monitoring decreases as the pupil moves from accretion which requires high teacher input to tuning or practical tasks. Moreover, it emphasises the complexity of learning processes and hence the intricacy of task analysis and design. Using this sequence, teachers can categorise tasks according to their appropriateness to the learner's position in the learning cycle Norman provides. Bennett *et al.* (1984) used a modification of Norman's three-phase analysis to categorise language and mathematics tasks set for 7 and 8 year-olds. They found that only 40 per cent of tasks in English and Mathematics set for 7 year-olds and 30 per cent of those set for 8 year-olds actually challenged children, despite teachers' concern to achieve a good 'match'. When the observations of Doyle are added to this analysis of task setting the situation becomes even more fraught. According to Doyle and Carter (1984), pupils and teachers engage in a process of negotiation around the setting and completion of tasks as part of the attempt to avoid the incipient chaos of classroom life. Pupils, they argue, try to reduce the risk of failure and consequent teacher displeasure by negotiating around the task until it can be seen as a set of routine activities. Moreover, teachers respond to pupils' bids or negotiations because of a similar need to maintain order and avoid chaos. Tasks are therefore modified and simplified to facilitate successful completion. The result is frequently an emphasis on routine responses. The observations of Watts and Bentley on the riskiness of self-exposure during effectual learning are also relevant to Doyle and Carter's thesis. Mismatch is therefore a complex issue in which cognition and affect appear to combine.

Bennett *et al.* (1984) found that more than half of the mathematical tasks they observed were mismatched to the children. Teachers tended to underestimate the ability of high-attaining children and overestimate that of the low attainers. The underestimated were unlikely to demand challenges as they safely and politely engaged in tasks that did not result in learning. Bennett and his colleagues suggest that classroom management issues are at the centre of some aspects of mismatch. We return to these points in Chapter 6.

What is most evident in the study by Bennett *et al.* (1984) is the inappropriate use of much learning time in classrooms. Teachers in their study were unable to find the time for diagnosis of pupil learning needs and lacked the skills for effective open-ended diagnostic assessment when they did. Questioning is clearly a problematic area as we have already indicated in Chapter 4 (Wood, 1988). Yet if we are to return to Vygotsky and the ZPD mentioned earlier in this chapter, it would seem that these skills should be a central part of the professional repertoire of teachers.[2]

Using memories

Of course, as we have already asserted, there is more to match than diagnosis. Again we return to Vygotsky and his emphasis on the organisation of pupils' learning. It would seem that for information to be processed and stored the child has to be able to 'make sense' of it.

Work on memory as a system of information processing and recall may help us to see the importance of sequencing and matching to the mental processing we term learning. Talking of adult learning, Craik and Tulving (1975) argued that the success of memory for items depended upon the degree to which they could be connected to other items already stored in the memory. Craik and Tulving were particularly concerned with what they termed the 'depth of processing' of information and suggested that information processing is facilitated by assisting the learner to make sense of new information by giving additional information about an item to be remembered. This assistance is termed 'elaboration' and its purpose seems to be to enable the learner to connect input to existing structures.[3]

In terms of teaching and learning it would seem that new information or skills need to be organised by teachers into manageable, relevant and carefully sequenced experiences for the learner. When dealing with children this is particularly problematic as the information store to which new inputs might be connected is more limited than that of most adults. Chi (1978 and 1981) argues that differences between adults and children in the ability to remember information are due largely to the fact that children have less content knowledge. Another element in the differences in processing is the fact that adults are more expert at using effective storage and retrieval strategies, i.e. they are better at organising information input.

The implications of Chi's work for teaching and learning are important. First, it enables teachers to regard the limitations of younger pupils as starting points for teaching. Children can be helped to become more expert in terms of content knowledge and in the organisation of their own learning. Secondly, and here we return to 'match', it emphasises the need to recognise that pupils do have more limited knowledge bases, and the necessity to sequence learning experiences which take these limitations into account and enable the child to 'make sense' in accord with teacher intentions.

Learning strategies

Attention to the organisation of the learning experiences to which the child is exposed would appear particularly important when dealing with novices, that is, when the learner has little expertise in the topic. Berliner (1987) differentiates between the information-processing abilities of novices and experts by noting that while the expert can select what is important from information received, novices are unable to separate the important from the unimportant. It would therefore seem that the three-stage task model offered by Norman (1978) provides a useful way of perceiving the role of the teacher. Learner expertise may be augmented by careful organisation of input whether that input is information, language or skills; or, more probably, a combination of these. Important aspects of the new experience are necessarily highlighted by the 'expert' teacher and pupils engage in processes of restructuring their existing storage system to accommodate the new information. They then progress to integrate that information or skill to the extent that its use becomes 'automatic'. The two stages described by Norman as restructuring and practice may well be positioned within independent problem-solving tasks set up by teachers. If we see problem-solving tasks as appropriate vehicles for the learner's internalisation of new experiences we need to recognise that it is important that pupils are in charge of their own learning at this stage. The adjustments being made relate to the knowledge structures of each individual child. While the teacher has set the goals for learning, and limited the opportunity for error by carefully organising input and by appropriate task setting and resourcing, the learner has to 'make sense' of it.

Teachers can, nevertheless, enhance the pupil's ability to make sense and make connections. Pupils can be taught to be better learners, better organisers of their own learning and better users of what they already know. At one level this is done through helping the learner to see the need to organise learning, to select what is important and to regulate and control related actions. At another level it is possible to teach children to recognise their need to exercise specific learning strategies.

Nisbet and Shucksmith (1986) have isolated strategies necessary for effective learning. These strategies are seen as 'executive processes' which select, regulate and apply skills to suit the needs of the task. Nisbet and Shucksmith describe learning to learn as developing metacognitive awareness or cultivating a 'seventh sense': an appreciation of one's own mental processes. Crucially, they see the learner's ability to monitor task demands and to select appropriate skills to be at the core of effective learning. Taking the notion of 'planfulness' as the key construct they explain the importance of enhancing the learner's ability to ask questions related to task demand, to reduce the task to manageable components, to monitor, check and revise progress towards the goal and, interestingly, to self-evaluate. They argue that enhancing the learner's ability to reflect upon his or her own learning and to respond to self-evaluations is an important teaching task enabling pupils to take responsibility for their own learning. The model of the self-evaluating learner is presented as a necessary partner to the self-evaluating teacher presented in earlier chapters.

To teach pupils to learn how to learn may, initially, appear a waste of valuable curriculum time but it would be argued that, conversely, the effort is an investment in more effective future learning. The processes can be integrated into much existing practice through an emphasis on planning and reviewing that is incorporated into task setting. The processes of learning demand considerable teacher support for the pupil, yet one aim of the secondary phase of schooling has to be to prepare pupils for independent study whether through project work in school or in further, post-school endeavours.

Notes and further reading

1. On Vygotskian approaches to learning, a good overview and introduction to Soviet Psychology is provided in Sutton (1983). These ideas are explored in greater depth in several papers in Wertsch (1984).

2. Examples of the developmental, interactional view of children's learning in and out of school are found in papers by Paul Light, David Wood, Peter Robinson, Chris Hensall and Jacqueline McGuire in Richards and Light (1986) and in an excellent collection of papers by Light *et al.* (1991). At a more specific level, Michael Beveridge's (1982) collection of papers on language and thought is challenging, as is Wells and Nicholls (1985), particularly the article by Terry Phillips (see Phillips 1985).

3. In the area of memory, an interesting approach has been taken by David Middleton and Derek Edwards as they examine remembering and forgetting as socially constituted. (See Middleton and Edwards, 1990.)

Seminar suggestions

1. Ask students to think of a typical classroom task that they have recently set a group of pupils, or would consider appropriate for a group.
   (a) Categorise this task as high or low risk – e.g.: Was it open ended? Were the goals clear? Were children able to evaluate their performance in the task? What was your role in task setting and evaluating their outcomes? What are the implications for planning and setting tasks?
   (b) Categorise this task according to the three levels of task demand offered by Norman (1978). What preceded it? What followed it? Is there a match between your task setting and Norman's framework? What are the implications for planning tasks and assessing pupils' performances?

2. Ask students to tape record themselves introducing a new object or materials to a boy and a girl. They may use the recording made for the activity suggested at the end of Chapter 4. Students should bring transcribed extracts from this recording to share at the seminar. Use these extracts to explore each student's own implicit theory of how learning occurs, for example: How important is language? How are children inducted into appropriate language use? What is the role of the adult? What theories of how pupils learn guide their actions as teachers? What proof do they have that these are useful theories?

3. Ask students to think of something they have completed recently, for example an essay, a sweater, a meal for friends. Ask them to analyse both

the task-specific skills, for example holding a pen, doing cable stitch, and the more general skills, for example clarifying aims, organising materials. Students should then compare the general skills, across tasks (reference to Nisbet and Shucksmith (1986) would be helpful here) and then discuss ways in which these may be taught in schools.

4. Ask students to examine carefully the two extended quotations from Bruner (1966) to be found in the section 'Theories of child development and theories of instruction' in this chapter. Discuss the implications of these statements for the role of the teacher of their subject.

CHAPTER 6

Classroom management

Keeping chaos at bay

Nobody could argue that teaching a class or even a group of children is easy. Teachers are faced with what might seem nigh impossible balancing acts. They need to ensure that children are motivated and confident enough to engage in constructing understandings of both the rituals of school and the official curriculum. At the same time teachers have to hold together these mentally and physically active individuals we term pupils as a cohesive and manageable group and succeed in leading them to learn a specific and prescribed body of knowledge and skills. If that were not enough, external sanctions are at work. At the very least a teacher must avoid having a 'noisy class', or forever be an uncomfortable reminder to colleagues of the potential chaos in every classroom. Additionally he or she must effectively carry the school's National Curriculum baton over the hurdles of appropriate levels of attainment. How does anyone manage it all?

Central to effective management is the ability to get the best from oneself and from others. When this maxim is applied to classrooms, the concern has to be use of pupil and teacher time so that children are able to learn efficiently and effectively. In other words, classroom management issues may start as questions about resources, uses of space and time and groupings of pupils, but at essence lies a concern with effective teaching and learning.

Models of classroom management will therefore reflect pedagogical practices. There is a process of double reflection at work here as equally pedagogical practices may be produced by models of classroom management, for example, lift-top sloping desks placed in rows do not lend themselves to practical group work activities, however much the teacher may wish to work in that way. Teachers have a range of management options available, though the choice is not always a free one, as schools develop particular styles into which pupils are inducted and within which the teaching staff are expected, by parents, pupils and colleagues, to operate.

There has been some considerable extension of the pedagogic demands made upon secondary teachers in the last twenty years. In addition to being experts in their subjects, they have had to master a range of teaching techniques and strategies. These are needed to suit the learning needs of a wide ability range of children and to provide a growing understanding of the complexities of the learning process seen, for example, in the introduction of flexible learning programmes. As a result, one lesson with a class may involve the teacher in exposition to the whole class, monitored group work on clearly defined tasks and one-to-one tutorial work. Or, conversely, another lesson may have involved the teacher in considerable pre-planning of activities, but with a minimal monitorial function for the duration of that particular session.

Styles of management may well have their provenance in the preferred interactional manner of each teacher, but are largely determined by his or her pedagogic stance (which may indeed be integral to interactional preferences), the immediate demands of the learning situation and the need to keep order. We shall look at the relationship between classroom management and pupil learning later in the chapter. Our initial focus will be the need to keep order. Three key issues are evident here: surveillance, busyness and negotiation.

Surveillance has always been a feature of traditional education as the teacher or lecturer stood in front of and facing students who listened and noted the wisdom imparted. With a move towards group and individual work and practical activity, surveillance becomes even more important as the teacher needs to monitor progress, and ensure that learners remain on task. The power of the surveyor is sustained only by his or her ability to see what is going on and hence to deny the right of private activity to the other actors, so ensuring that order and official purposes are maintained. The surveillance model can only be operated within classrooms in which an interactive pedagogy is dominant if the teacher engages in careful organisation of space, resources and time. The teacher needs to be able to observe each child at work with at best a sweep of the head or at most movement by a few paces. Resources need to be organised and positioned so that self-selection by children may be noted even at a distance, and time needs to be apportioned to groups of children in blocks which ensure that monitoring of some groups may occur while more intensive teaching is going on with others.

In many subjects this is not easy to arrange and rooms have to be used for multiple purposes and a variety of teaching strategies. At the same time stringent timetabling provides a dominating constraint. But, as we shall see later, the teacher as all-seeing ringmaster or mistress is an important concept.

Busyness has its roots in two apparently contradictory strands in the development of educational practice. The first strand has its roots in the emphasis placed on 'work' within protestant culture. The high moral value accorded the work ethic is best summarised in the fear of the fun the devil might have with idle-handed children. Compulsory schooling, with its original role of ensuring the moral well-being of the poorer classes, clearly had to ensure that the sin or idleness was not evident. The second starting point, apparently in stark contrast to the first, is found in the belief in childhood innocence, underpinning the progressive movement of the 1930s that was eventually taken up in the Plowden Report (CACE, 1967). In this strand, the child's natural curiosity is believed to motivate him or her to act upon the world and so learn. These arguments are elaborated in the infant school context by Walkerdine (1984). They are nonetheless of current relevance in secondary schooling with the increased emphasis placed there on active learning across the curriculum. White's (1959) theory of 'effectiveness motivation' provides a bridge between the power of the child's 'natural' curiosity and the demands of a specific curriculum, as he argues that children are motivated to undertake tasks at which they feel they will be effective. As a result, pupils' natural behaviour is channelled into a specific curriculum through appropriate matching of task to child. Evidence of successful task setting is seen in the 'busyness' of the pupil as he or she is engaged on a task. In both strands the learner's engagement with a classroom task is a visible sign of teacher success in managing children.

In terms of the reality of coping with the learning needs of thirty or more pupils, task setting and learners' time on task are crucial classroom management issues, since unoccupied children or adolescents are poised to trigger the incipient chaos of classroom life already discussed in Chapter 5. Teachers tend to organise their teaching day as a series of tasks or pupil activities. Nevertheless, in their study of task allocation and matching of task and child in top infant classes and first-year junior classes, Bennett *et al.* (1984) found that the 'experienced and able' teachers they observed had problems in achieving appropriate match. Watts and Bentley (1987) also suggest that match is not easily achieved at secondary level. Bennett's team also noted that mismatch was caused by both underestimation as well as overestimation. A simple measure of time on task may give some indication of a teacher's success as a manager of children. But as Bennett and Blundell (1983) point out, the relationship between pupil involvement and achievement may be positive, but it is variable, ranging from correlations of 0.1 to 0.6. He notes that classroom observation suggests that the issue is more complex than time spent at work. What needs to be taken into account is the quality of that time, which is maximised by the appropriate match of child to the learning experience. In turn this is achieved by careful task setting.

Interestingly, Bennett *et al.* (1984) explained that teachers tended to be unaware of the mismatch observed by the research team because of various processes of negotiation at work. Teachers eager to keep order tended to praise children for following procedures rather than for understanding. Children politely worked on tasks that did not challenge them, while low attainers often spent much of their time waiting in queues for teacher attention.

This finding is corroborated in a US study with secondary age pupils. Doyle (1986) noted that in one US study high-achieving students spent twice as much time on task as low-achieving pupils and completed three times as much work. While it might appear obvious that time on task is related to achievement, the relationship is far from simple in classrooms, as pupils can be taken off task because of their need for guidance. West and Wheldall (1989) observed children waiting for teacher attention in twenty infant school classrooms and found that although the average waiting time was 84 seconds, in a quarter of the classrooms waiting time could exceed 10 minutes and children were also observed to 'give up' waiting. West and Wheldall found that operating a mobile queue system was more effective than expecting children to sit in their places and raise their hands, but they stress the need for further research in this area.

While West and Wheldall do not examine the reasons for demands for teacher attention, it would be fairly safe to assume that 'the queue' is made up of those children who need direct help and those who require teacher attention perhaps for procedural checks in mathematics, or spelling in language activities. As a result the less able are more likely to spend more time off task. Ways of dealing with demands on teacher time will be discussed later in this chapter.

It appears that pupil 'busyness' on task and teacher planning of pupil tasks are central classroom control issues. Nevertheless it is important to note that activity on task cannot always be equated with children's learning, as quite complex processes of negotiation also centre around pupil performance on task and teacher task setting.

Negotiation that is flexible yet goal-orientated is an essential management skill. Within classrooms this skill helps to explain how tasks are implemented by teachers and interpreted by pupils in ways which ensure that order is maintained. While surveillance and 'busyness' explain classroom order in terms of control features, examination of negotiations allows exploration of the processes underpinning the management of learning.

As we have already discussed in Chapter 4, children are inducted into the rules and rituals of classroom life at the start of each academic year. Once the rules of 'being a pupil' have been accepted as the framework for pupil behaviour, a more focused form of negotiation appears to occur around classroom tasks. Here the observations of Doyle discussed in Chapters 4 and 5 are particularly helpful as they clearly relate classroom order to pupil learning (see Doyle (1986) for an overview). As we have already outlined, he argues that tasks which are challenging to pupils because they demand a demonstration of understanding of topics, and because this may be open ended in nature, are perceived as ambiguous by pupils. As a result children try to limit the riskiness of the demands by requesting more information and so lessen the cognitive challenge of the task. If pupils demand less ambiguity and fail to achieve it by successful negotiation with the teacher they may react with disruptive behaviour in order to avoid the task by other means. The success of pupils in negotiating down the level of task demand and the importance of keeping order sometimes leads experienced teachers to decide to omit more challenging tasks from their repertoire and so limit the learning experiences available to their pupils by concentrating, as Bennett *et al.* (1984) noted, on the procedural rather than the more cognitively challenging aspects of tasks.

These observations of the negotiation processes may not square either with the description of schooling as cultural transmission through the curriculum, or with the interactive model of learning presented in Chapter 5. There is obviously a need for the teacher to resolve the tensions and to ensure that children's learning of the curriculum is optimised. One method may simply lie in clearer goal setting for more risky or open-ended tasks. In their examination of learning strategies, Nisbet and Shucksmith (1986) suggest that the clear explanation of goals to pupils is a prerequisite to pupil use of effective learning strategies as pupils are then able to assess and select ways of achieving these goals. Here the pedagogic emphasis is shifted from products to processes, pupil self evaluation is encouraged and the risk of failing to achieve the correct solution is minimised.[1]

Behavioural approaches in teaching

Another angle on classroom management can be seen in the Behavioural Approach to Teaching Secondary Aged Pupils (BATSACK) developed by Merrett and Wheldall (1988). Their work aims to induct secondary teachers into what they describe as 'positive' responses to children's behaviour through a school-based in-service training programme. The focus is on classroom management. Teachers are taught to examine the antecedents to pupil behaviour and, by selecting appropriate behavioural responses themselves, to provide positive reinforcement or encouragement for specifically defined pupil behaviours.

An enormous amount of research on behavioural approaches to teaching has been carried out in North America, and they have also had considerable influence in Britain. Their theoretical underpinning is in learning theory, and in the assumption that the same principles govern the 'learning' of behaviour as of any other task. Thus, if children enjoy receiving their teacher's attention, the teacher can use attention selectively as a way of increasing the frequency of particular behaviours. The behaviour may be working on a maths problem, cooperating with other pupils or sitting down except when invited to move around the classroom: the same reinforcement principles apply.

Educational psychologists often provide 'behavioural' or 'behaviour modification' programmes to help teachers cope with difficult or disruptive behaviour. Typically, such programmes have six stages (see Table 6.1).[2] The evidence for the effectiveness of behavioural approaches is contentious (see Berger, 1982). On the other hand, evaluations of BATPACK, the primary version of BATSACK, have reported changes in teacher behaviour, with evidence that positive reinforcement of appropriate pupil behaviour does help teachers in managing pupils, at least in the short to medium term (Merrett and Wheldall, 1990)

Table 6.1 **Stages of a typical behavioural programme**

1. Teacher identifies behaviour or skill which he/she wishes the class or a particular child to acquire (or, in the case of behaviour, to modify).
2. Obtain 'base-line' against which to measure subsequent progress. This is done by recording the frequency of the target behaviour.
3. Analyse antecedents, or events which precede the target behaviour, and consequences, or events which follow it. This should show what is acting as a stimulus and/or as a reinforcement for the target behaviour.
4. Using reinforcement principles, plan a programme to achieve the desired objective.
5. Put the programme into practice, maintaining records so as to evaluate progress against the base-line measures.
6. After reviewing progress, modify or develop the programme as necessary.

Nevertheless, two cautionary points should be made about the use of behavioural approaches. First, Wheldall (1982) has warned against 'behavioural overload', or the use of unnecessarily 'heavy', and perhaps primitive techniques to deal with relatively minor problems. In a similar vein, Berger (1979) warned of the danger of a 'mindless technology', and in a later article argued that 'classroom problems are influenced by a complex set of factors interacting and changing over time', and not simply by 'the behaviour of teachers or peers' (Berger, 1982, p. 292).

These could be regarded as essentially technical points, resulting from inappropriate use of behavioural principles. Yet the second point is more complex and challenges one of the behaviourists' most fundamental assumptions: that effective teaching depends on clear and precise specification of objectives. It is difficult to imagine teaching successfully without having clear objectives. Yet, admitting that objectives are necessary to effective teaching does not mean that they are sufficient. McNamara (1988) has identified seven standard objections to an over-reliance on objectives (see also Eisner (1985)).

1. The rationale for selecting objectives is often unclear.

2. The detail with which objectives can be specified varies unacceptably from subject to subject: what precise objective must be met on the path to producing a creative, original story?
3. Splitting a curricular task into objectives can trivialise it: 'when we move on to pupils deploying their analytical and critical skills we simply cannot talk in terms of objectives' (McNamara, 1988, p. 41).
4. Specifying objectives generates either too few or too many. Unless the number is kept artificially low, children will learn far more in the course of a week than the teacher can specify as behavioural objectives.
5. The more varied and stimulating the curricular activities, the more difficult it becomes to obtain agreement on whether objectives have been achieved.
6. Whatever and however we teach, we convey attitudes through the hidden curriculum: 'The hidden curriculum which is associated with the objectives approach seems to have little to commend it' (p. 42).
7. In however much detail objectives are specified, we still have to face questions about *how* we achieve them.

This said, it remains true that appropriateness of reinforcement is necessary for effective classroom management. Children are unlikely to respond well to teachers who appear uninterested in their efforts and unresponsive to their interests. Most teachers use reinforcement principles intuitively, but the evidence suggests that this is more frequently directed at appropriate educational tasks than at appropriate behaviour (Merrett and Wheldall, 1986). In other words, teachers seem to have difficulty in reinforcing 'good' behaviour, and may inadvertently encourage disruptive behaviours by directing their attention to the children concerned.

Classroom management and pupil learning

At a more general level, the tension between cognitive challenge and classroom disorder may best be resolved through a greater emphasis on strategic planning, as disorder needs to be prevented rather than cured. From this it follows that the negotiation system should be sustained as breakdown would lead to disorder. The teacher's management role becomes one of creating operating systems for classroom groups which are clearly related to pupil task demands. Classroom rules need to be directly related to the support of pupils who are engaged in learning activities. Put more simply, the needs of pupils while on task and while changing task need to be anticipated in the organisation and resourcing of the classroom. Classrooms need to be structured and rules agreed so that the support of pupils' active engagement on tasks over a maximum period of time, is the central issue. At a practical level this may mean, as examples, eliminating from the 'queue' those children who need to move on to the next task or to have access to a piece of equipment or careful resourcing of a problem-solving task. Again Doyle's (1986) analysis of classroom life is particularly helful as it places an emphasis on the relationship between pupil learning and classroom management. This is because a coherent management system needs to be underpinned by a particular set of beliefs about what pupils need to learn and about how they best learn. The focus on pupil engagement on task and on interaction with resources and teachers, allows us to recognise the relevance of Doyle's observations to the view of pupil learning described in Chapter 5.

Clearly there is more to classroom management than preventing chaos. Children attend school in order to learn. A system of classroom management that takes the learning needs of pupils as its starting point has clear advantages over one that is overly influenced by, for example, school traditions. The levels of task demand noted by Norman (1978), and outlined in Chapter 5, provide a useful link to relate pupils' learning needs to resourcing and use of teacher time. This link ensures that management issues spring from the assessment of pupils, an understanding of how pupils learn and a structured view of the relationship between tasks and the curriculum.

Using such a framework, the planning of the learning process starts with an assessment of the learning needs of groups of pupils, which is based upon their previous performances.

For management purposes these needs can be categorised in two ways. First, one can consider them in terms of the amount of teacher time they demand, for example, in introducing new ideas, in monitoring learners as they start to make sense of a topic on their own or in small groups, or in resourcing their independent activity or practice tasks. Each type of activity demands specific resourcing and a varying amount of teacher time. The introduction of a new skill demands considerable pupil–teacher interaction; making sense of new knowledge and trying out an existing skill may only need careful resourcing and teacher monitoring, while practice tasks may require careful prior resourcing but minimal teacher class time and much pupil self-direction. In some teaching situations practitioners will be able to group children so that, throughout the teaching session, high demand teacher time is required by only one group at a time. Those pupils not requiring teacher attention would, in those circumstances, be engaged on tasks requiring only monitoring or on practice tasks. This method of classroom management may well provide the key to the success of mixed ability teaching.[3]

If, however, timetable or other resource constraints restrict the management options available, it is still important to consider the learning needs of the pupils in terms of the demands of the tasks or experiences with which they are provided. It is clearly important to understand that exposition or demonstrations need to be followed by opportunities for trial and error in order to accommodate and make sense of the new information. This has to occur before pupils move on to practice skills or use knowledge in perhaps the form of essay writing or complex problem solving. It is the middle 'making sense' stage of the cycle we outlined, that is frequently given insufficient consideration. One way of ensuring that a greater emphasis is placed on opportunities for making sense of trial and error is through the use of interactive group work in the cycle of pupil learning experiences.

Groups and grouping

Interactive group work seems seldom to be a feature of British classrooms, despite the popularity of grouping as an organisational strategy (for example, see Bennett (1985a) and Yeomans (1983) for overviews of research in this area). Clearly arranging pupils into working groups does not ensure that the pupils interact and engage cooperatively on tasks.

Yet it does seem to be the case that cooperative group work that is designed to allow the pupils to express, and hence test, their own ideas and to discuss the current focus of classwork aids mastery and retention of new information and is motivating for the pupils concerned (Johnson and Johnson, 1982). Nevertheless, this form of interaction is not easy to establish. Phillips (1985) argues that group work that is based on practical activities does not produce the language that establishes the patterns of reflective consideration essential to the learning process. He suggests that, in what he describes as the 'operational mode' of discourse, children who are engaged on practical tasks are fixed in the present and the literal and are involved in 'decision making in action'. As a result, action rather than reflection is the dominant theme. In contrast the 'hypothetical mode', he notes, encourages discussion and review. This mode is marked by cues such as 'what about', 'what if' and the use of 'could' or 'might'. It is more rarely found in classrooms and, it would seem, requires emphasis through the timetabling of *post hoc* discussions in which groups of pupils review and reflect upon tasks. These tasks need not be entirely practical; recently the second author has worked with teachers who have encouraged their pupils to review and reflect upon audio tapes of their own discussions in GCSE literature and language sessions. In addition to enabling the pupil to take time to test personal hypotheses in what Watts and Bentley (1987) describe as 'non-threatening learning environments' (see Chapter 5), the processes of review and reflection encourage the learner autonomy, which is increasingly important for sixth form and later studies.

Developing learner autonomy

As we have already indicated, the model of supported self-study which was developed within the Technical and Vocational Educational Initiative (TVEI) would seem to fit well with the management and learning processes suggested in this chapter. At the same time it produces important implications for the management of people, time and of resources to support pupil learning. Supported self-study, or flexible learning within TVEI, aims to meet the learning needs of students 'through the flexible management and use of a range of learning activities, environments and resources' and to increase students' responsibility for their own learning 'within a framework of appropriate support' (Trayers, 1989).

The learning cycle proposed is that of negotiation of goals, experience of task, reflection and review. Student learning needs and goals are identified through negotiation so that student and curricular targets are matched. At the task or experience stage pupils take on considerable responsibility for planning and organising the activity. In addition, they make direct use of resources supplied by teachers. These resources may include data bases, libraries, or other people. Reflection occurs in tutorials with teachers and other pupils and review allows joint evaluation of the activity from aims to outcome and may be included in the profile assessment of the pupil. Reviews may also be used as the basis for further target setting.

Pupil involvement in both target setting and evaluation is an essential component in any teaching programme that aims to enhance the autonomy of the individual learner (see Edwards, 1988). There is always an inherent tension in matching curricular demands with pupil autonomy and it is here that the teacher's management skills are tested.

Within the flexible learning model available under TVEI the role of the teacher is very different from that of the subject specialist who endeavours to pass on knowledge; instead he or she is required to create relationships of trust with pupils as goals are negotiated and progress reviewed. The teacher should stand back while pupils undertake the task or experience a stage alone or in groups; in addition the teacher must carefully resource the learning experiences so that personal learning and curricular needs are met. Pupils should be allowed the time and space to contribute to discussions in which the focus is the pupils' experience rather than the teacher's knowledge. Teachers are therefore required to exercise complex management skills as prerequisites to enabling pupils to take on subject knowledge.

The management of people

An essential component in the management of pupils on flexible learning cycles is understanding between pupil and teacher. Elsewhere,

Powell (1985) has described this as 'teacher sensitivity'. Powell reminds us that the most important skill in management is 'to be able to see situations through the eyes of those one is seeking to manage'. That this skill is also crucial to that of assessing pupil learning needs and target setting, and to the joint evaluation of progress, should already be evident. Salmon and Claire (1984) premised their study of classroom collaboration on Kelly's personal construct psychology (Bannister and Fransella, 1971). In Salmon and Claire's study the frames of reference which direct pupils' and teachers' actions were explored to discover commonality or similarity. Personal construct psychology informs us that the individual's frames of reference are constructed from the sets of anticipations and interpretations placed on events by each participant. Each will create his or her own construct system or framework through which experiences are filtered and opportunities for learning are shaped. As we have already indicated in Chapter 5 with reference to the work of Watts and Bentley (1987), teachers need to access these constructions in order to diagnose learning needs and ways forward. Salmon and Claire suggest that accessing pupil understanding is also a crucial element in the management of that learning and we would argue that it is essential to the success of any learning cycle.

The management of time

For many secondary school teachers this is both a major issue and one over which they have little control. Professional decision making is constrained by timetable demands which have their provenance in a combination of administrative convenience and traditional exposition models of teaching. Nevertheless, teachers do have to consider two important elements of the management of time. First, they need to ensure that time they spend in contact with pupils is used well. Care needs to be taken in analysing task demands and the ways in which the pupils have responded to these demands, and in encouraging pupil discussion of these in order to ensure that they learn through their own reflections on the experiences. Consequently, time spent with pupils demands careful preparation and freedom from competing demands, perhaps from other groups. Secondly, and equally, the quality of pupils' use of time merits continuous review. Time on task may be a useful starting point, leading to a consideration of ways in which time is wasted (for example, by waiting for teacher attention), but is a relatively low-level measure of pupil involvement when compared with the importance of the quality of the experience. Here management issues connect squarely with pupil learning around the notion of appropriate match of task and learner.

No clear and simple guidelines for ensuring effective use of teacher time can be given as each classroom and series of tasks may demand a variety of strategies. The first step is to recognise the importance of time management and to review how time is spent. Once more we return to the Action Research methods of self-review mentioned in Chapter 1 in order to provide baseline data on which decisions for improved time management may be made. It may be helpful to keep an informal diary for a day or so to consider time use; or a simple checklist of questions may be more appropriate (see Table 6.2).

Each teacher's individual profile would provide starting points for further action. This action might be, for example, the implementation of review sessions for the whole class to feedback, evaluate and set standards of work. A result of this could be to eliminate from the queue some of the pupils who constantly seem to await approval from the teacher. Other examples might be the shifting of more responsibility for equipment to the children or the end of marking alongside the learner.

Within the framework of the interactive style of pedagogy we advocate it is difficult to separate use of teacher time from pupil time. Flexible learning is but one manifestation of this pedagogy. Clear goal setting to reduce a fear of risk taking complements an emphasis on process goals – for example, planning, selecting and evaluating. The match of task and learner is pivotal and has been discussed in Chapter 5, but careful assessment of pupil performance on task necessarily underpins future task setting and is more likely to ensure a higher quality engagement on task. At a very practical level, when pupils feel that they 'own' the classroom's learning resources, when they have a clear idea of how much work is expected in each session, their autonomy is increased and many of the more mundane demands on teacher attention are removed. This allows more opportunity for the teacher to focus on children's thinking and learning. Management of time is therefore explicitly related to the management of resources.

Table 6.2 **A 'use of time' teacher prompt list**

Interactions with other adults:	Head of department
	Other colleagues
	Parents
	Domestic staff
	Others, e.g. students
Domestic chores undertaken:	e.g. finding materials
	giving out equipment
Main activities with children:	List:

The management of resources

Given that time in classrooms is frequently organised by teachers in terms of tasks for learners, the resourcing of these activities requires detailed attention. Careful prior resourcing limits options available to the learner, helping to ensure that the pupil faces challenges and can avoid easier, already well-practised, solutions. Equally, careful preparation of materials releases the teacher for work with pupils while they are on task and helps eliminate the more mundane questions relating to starting tasks. Within the learning cycle suggested earlier in this chapter, careful resourcing of pupils' experiences would be considered crucial to the second or 'making sense' level of the learning experience. The absentee teacher is still very much in control of the pupils' curricular activities, yet able to focus his or her interactions on the immediate learning needs of other learners. This aspect of the teacher's role is also necessarily very much to the fore in many flexible learning strategies. Equally, a consequence of the high value to be placed on teacher time is the need to consider ways in which the classroom may become self-running. Methods include giving specific responsibilities to individual pupils and training all pupils in group responsibilities. However, in terms of materials it necessitates ensuring the accessibility of resources and instructions for tasks. Yet again each professional needs to consider each situation: for example, how much time is wasted asking permission to use equipment or receive appropriate material? What kind of follow-up 'making sense' or practice activities could be written out on work cards and kept in a small box readily available for that odd five or ten minutes for early finishers?

Giving pupils the right to use materials with the consequent responsibility for their final selection and, within a clear framework, the right to select tasks, may be an important step forward in freeing the teacher to act as professional pedagogue. Classroom management strategies can only be justified by their capacity to facilitate pupils' learning.

Notes and further reading

1. Ways in which control is negotiated in classrooms have been a research focus in the sociology of education over the last two decades. Interesting papers can be found in the following collections: Woods and Hammersley (1977); Woods (1980a); and Woods (1980b).
2. Useful introductions to the use of applied behaviour analysis in the classroom can be found in Harrop (1983) and Wheldall and Glynn (1989). For a reader containing many of the seminal articles on classroom behaviour modification, see O'Leary and O'Leary (1979).
3. For a discussion of research on mixed ability reading, see Gregory (1984).

Seminar suggestions

1. Ask students to consider their current classroom, or one in which they have recently worked. Ask them to draw a plan of the classroom, placing furniture and display areas as they currently stand. As a first-stage activity students can discuss, in pairs, the rationale or justification for existing use of space. Points to be considered could include the importance of surveillance, busyness and negotiation. Remaining in the same pairings, a second-stage activity could involve students in examining ways in which the layout might be changed in the light of some of the points raised by this chapter.

2. Prior to the seminar ask each student to monitor or observe one child for a period of up to 20 minutes, noting as much as possible of what he or she is doing on a minute-by-minute basis. A pro forma might help, for example:

Time in minutes	Child's actions	Additional notes
11.01		
11.02		
11.03		

Ask students to analyse the information to consider how much time was spent on task. The seminar discussion could focus on how that time might be increased and on the importance of the quality of the task and the level of engagement.

3. Ask students to work alone to think of one 'typical' teaching day from the moment they arrive until they leave school at the end of the day. Ask them to list, in chronological order when possible, the activities a teacher undertakes, e.g. prepare resources, collect equipment, give out paper, move desks, talk with colleagues, listen to pupil problems, run discussion group. Ask them to work in pairs to categorise these activities. You may want to suggest your own categories, but the following may be useful starting points: 'could be delegated to children', 'important for children's thinking and learning', 'important for children's social and emotional development', 'not a productive use of time'. Some activities may fall in several categories.

    Discuss as a group (a) how teacher time might be used most productively and (b) how the less productive activities may be curtailed or delegated, perhaps to pupils as educationally valuable activities.

CHAPTER 7

Personal and social education

Introduction

Most secondary school prospectuses contain a commitment to the 'all-round development' of their pupils. Primary teachers sometimes used to say that this claim was needed to counteract the excessively subject-orientated nature of the secondary curriculum. This cynical claim is less often heard today with the introduction of the National Curriculum and its associated attainment targets in primary schools. Nevertheless, the commitment to pupil's 'all-round' development clearly reflects the view that secondary schools should be doing more than transmit culturally approved knowledge and skills. As schools market themselves in search of pupils, they aim to persuade parents of the strength of their commitment to matters such as dress, behaviour and social responsibility as well as academic standards and examination results. There is also a growing professional consensus that schools should be preparing pupils for the choices and challenges of life outside the school. Hence, topics such as careers education, health education and moral education should be addressed in a more systematic way than was formerly considered necessary.

Certainly, there can be few schools, if any, that do not claim a commitment to their pupils' well-being that extends beyond their progress in the National Curriculum. Nor can there be many that deny a fundamental commitment to personal and social education. Yet the meaning of personal and social education in terms of curriculum planning and the day-to-day classroom practice remains tantalisingly unclear. This chapter aims to unravel what may be meant by personal and social education and to consider its practical implications for secondary school and classroom practice. We shall start by examining the concept of personal and social education (PSE) and its aims, and shall consider some of the tensions to which they give rise. We shall then move to the curricular implications, and finally to the school's relationship with its pupils' parents, and the impact this may have on the pupils' development.

Concept and aims of personal and social education

The inevitability of personal and social education

Even if they wanted to, teachers could not avoid having an impact on pupils' personal and social development. Children develop as members of social groups: the family, playgroup, school and so on. As we have argued throughout the book, this involves a process of mutual adaptation. At school, children adapt to their teacher's expectations, either by behaving in the accepted way or, occasionally, otherwise. This adaptation process entails that they learn from the way the school is organised and from their teacher's response to different situations. They will learn about power relationships from their teacher's behaviour towards them, *and* from observation of the interaction between different members of staff. What tasks, for example, are senior women teachers expected to undertake compared with men? Are disagreements evident between senior teachers or between senior teachers and teachers in the main professional grade? In a more obvious way, perhaps, pupils learn, for better or worse, what their teachers consider to be suitable behaviour, dress and activities for boys and for girls. To illustrate the inevitability of personal and social education, consider three situations:

1. When discussing nicknames with her tutor group of 12 to 13 year-olds a newly qualified teacher notices a group of boys giggling and trying to attract the attention of another boy, Peter, who is obviously angry and embarrassed. One of the giggling group eventually explains that Peter's nickname is 'Gayboy'.
2. A teacher hears a 12 year-old boy mutter, 'fuck it' as the class settles down at the start of the lesson. A month later the same teacher hears the same expletive from a girl, this time in the playground.
3. A fight starts in the mid-morning playtime. A Bangladeshi boy says that he has been called names, and that he's going to 'get' the name-callers. Further investigation reveals that the name calling is racist in nature.

We do not wish to consider here how the teacher should react to these incidents. Each of them, though, is likely to be familiar to experienced teachers. Our point is simply that children will learn *something* from the teacher's reaction, irrespective of what this reaction may be.

Defining personal and social education

Elsewhere personal and social education is defined as all learning experiences from which pupils derive:

a developing sense of their own abilities and of their rights and responsibilities as contributing members of the school and of the wider community in which they live. (Galloway, 1990a, p. 10)

By a 'developing' sense of their rights and responsibilities we imply simply that pupils' concepts of themselves and of their position in their family, school and society develop with age. How the concept of self develops is the school's responsibility as well as the parents', though tension is likely when parents and teachers differ in their views of the school's role. Many of the learning experiences which affect pupils' personal and social development are incidental, arising from the school's hidden curriculum. We shall nevertheless argue that personal and social education has important implications for classroom management. It also has implications for the curriculum which require careful planning as part of the National Curriculum. At this stage we need to look at issues arising from our definition of personal and social education and at some of the problems arising from it.[1]

Whose rights and responsibilities?

Logically, we cannot talk about children developing a sense of their rights and responsibilities as contributing members of the school without also considering our own rights and responsibilities as teachers. Asking what children, or their parents, should feel entitled to expect from school is perhaps one of the most effective ways of getting ourselves in deep water. Diener and Dweck (1978) have argued that children develop 'learned helplessness' when they feel that teachers are criticising them as individuals, rather than criticising aspects of their performance on a specific task. Helping them to see why they are finding something difficult, whether it be learning to read or grasping a new concept in mathematics, is perhaps one of the most challenging tasks for a teacher. Too often children interpret what teachers say to them or write in their books ('critical feedback' in the jargon) as a comment on their own ability rather than as a way of helping them to master the task in hand.[2]

Values and beliefs

Whenever we state what standard we expect from pupils – for example, in dress or behaviour – we are influenced by our own values and beliefs. The problem here is that each teacher's own beliefs and values will certainly differ from those of many pupils and their parents.

Two examples of beliefs are: 'There is but one God, Allah', and 'Jesus is Lord'. Two examples of values are: 'We should respect the religious beliefs of others', and 'We should not make fun of people because they are disabled'. Differences in religious and political belief may be associated with differences in values. Most Quakers, for example, would argue that war is never morally justified. This is a value judgement, derived from their belief that the biblical injunction to turn the other cheek proscribes violence in any circumstances. Other Christian groups do not share this belief, and consequently adopt different values.

In spite of the interrelationship between values and beliefs, it remains true that no community can flourish without broad agreement on values. Lack of such agreement leads inevitably to anarchy. Any school or children's organisation requires a generally agreed, though not immutable, set of values in order to maintain a climate of stability in which learning is possible. It also requires some concept of its own interrelationship with wider groups. Yet as we have already argued, teachers are not free agents. Through successive Education Acts, the government is encouraging a particular set of values. In their visits of inspection, HMI take a keen interest in the school's philosophy and social climate. Parents may impose values on a school, for example commitment to uniformity of dress, by means of an implicit threat to send their children elsewhere. It follows that the values that the head and staff seek to promote throughout a school cannot be totally idiosyncratic. If they are rejected, or just not understood, by a majority of parents, no policy on personal and social education is likely to be effective. Another influence, which is still of some importance, is that of the LEA. Just as the teacher's values are reflected in the written and unwritten policies of the school, so the collective values of the Education Committee may also be formalised into a set of more or less well-defined policies that attempt to influence the values adopted and promoted by teachers.

Notable examples in recent years are anti-racism and anti-sexism policies. Some LEAs have requested each school to produce its own policy for combating racism and sexism. It is important to note that the assumed need for a formal policy to combat these problems implies that the teachers' existing value systems may tolerate, or even foster, behaviour that discriminates against pupils or fellow staff members on the basis of race or sex. The success of an anti-racist or anti-sexist policy at LEA level in overcoming racist or sexist practices in schools remains a matter for research. What is not in doubt is that what pupils learn in school about personal relationships, with each other and with adults, will be influenced by their perception of their teachers' values. The ways in which these are formulated and expressed will be reflected in the schools' climate and hidden curriculum.

The most far-reaching attempt to influence the values that schools seek to develop has not, however, come from LEAs but from central government in the form of the 1988 Education Act. The introduction of a national curriculum places an explicit value on an organised and centrally determined body of knowledge, while national testing seeks to develop a competitive ethos within and between schools. The increase in parents' freedom to select their children's school, their greater representation on governing bodies and the local financial management of schools may all be seen as an attempt to increase a sense of parental and community responsibility for what happens in schools.

Tensions in personal and social education

Care and control: educational policy issues

No country could afford to be unconcerned about the impact of schooling on children's personal and social development. There is no system of government in which politicians could truthfully say: 'We have neither concern nor responsibility for the values, knowledge and skills that our children develop.' Education, then, can never be apolitical. The origins of compulsory state education in Britain are sometimes thought to lie in an altruistic concern for the plight of young children in the factories and mines and in the growing belief that education was intrinsically humanising and liberating. Sadly, the evidence to support this cosily benevolent view is rather limited. A more realistic appraisal sees the introduction of compulsory education for all as a way of socialising children into accepting their 'rightful' place in society by teaching them the values they would need as acceptable employees in late nineteenth- and early twentieth-century industrial society.[3]

In democracies and in totalitarian states teachers are subject to pressure over both the official and the hidden curriculum. The nature and strength of the pressure varies widely, depending on whether those in power regard the current status quo as acceptable. In Britain a liberal view of education went largely unchallenged for some thirty years after the Second World War. This saw education as intrinsically desirable for its own sake with little reason to doubt that schools would produce young people with the attitudes and skills needed to play a useful part in society. Both the Newsome Report on secondary education (Ministry of Education, 1963) and the Plowden Report on primary education (CACE, 1967) lent powerful support to this view with their commitment to child-centred learning and their belief in the school's contribution in mitigating the effects of social disadvantage.

The rhetoric of liberal education suited teachers since it allowed them extensive control over the curriculum. At a time of low unemployment and increasing prosperity it also suited successive governments. Sociologists and psychologists could draw attention to inequality within the education system, as well as within society, arguing for example that it merely equipped 'working class kids for working class jobs' (Willis, 1977), but as long as most people had jobs and living standards continued to rise schools remained relatively free from political attention. The fact that over 12 per cent of pupils left school with no formal qualification (Fontana, 1984) was of little political importance.

James Callaghan signalled that all this was changing in a speech at Ruskin College in 1976, thereby unleashing a debate that led ultimately to the 1988 Education Reform Act. A combination of factors created increasing political interest in education. They included rising unemployment, the growing power of the unions, the decline of traditional industries with their demand for unskilled or semi-skilled labour, technological changes with consequent demand for new skills, and the growth of smaller industries requiring a more specialised and more adaptable workforce. In this climate the traditional liberal curriculum appeared out-dated, posing a threat to the country's economic prosperity. More important, if large numbers of pupils continued to leave school with no marketable skills and no prospect of employment the stability of the country would be threatened.

It was not enough, though, to introduce a national curriculum. At least as important, teachers had to expect more of children, and parents had to expect more of teachers. In educational jargon, the liberal view of education gave way to an instrumental one, in which schools and colleges were seen as an instrument for social change. The ethos of liberal education for some and learning to labour for others was replaced by the enterprise culture for all, at least in political rhetoric. The impact of an increasingly vocational orientation in the curriculum affected all sectors of the education system. In the secondary schools it was seen in the introduction of work experience, in many schools for all pupils, and the appointment of careers education specialists. It was also seen in the appointment of representatives from local industry and commerce to governing bodies. At the same time HMI started to take an interest in schools' links with industry and teacher training courses had to satisfy a committee appointed by the Secretary of State that they were equipping students to develop their pupils' knowledge and understanding of the world of work (DES, 1989a).

Psychology and personal and social education

The political attention to education throughout the 1980s was explicitly motivated by interest in the personal qualities that schools should, according to the government, be developing in their pupils. This raises questions about the contribution that psychology makes to the theory and practice of personal and social education. It should by now be clear that psychology can never tell teachers what is 'appropriate' personal and social education, nor can it specify with any authority the aims or scope of personal and social education. Psychologists do claim to tell us what concepts children can grasp at different ages. This has obvious implications for understanding children's moral development, though even here there is controversy between different schools of thought. Returning to our definition of personal and social education, psychology cannot tell us what are appropriate rights and responsibilities for children of different ages since these are culturally or politically determined. The conservative government of the 1980s appeared to see the function of personal and social education as preparing young people to take their place as responsible citizens and employees (DES, 1985). This does not always rest comfortably with the more liberal tradition of creating questioning, critical, autonomous young people who think and act for themselves, willing 'to resist exploitation, to innovate and to be vigilant in the defence of liberty', as was recognised in a joint DES/HMI document in 1977. It is worth noting that the concept of personal and social education was considered at least as important in Hitler's Germany as in any late twentieth-century western democracy. Our point is that while different people may agree on the importance of personal and social education, they may have entirely different things in mind, depending on their political, moral and religious values.

Care and control: school and classroom policy

Rabinowitz (1981) drew an interesting parallel between the experience of secondary school pupils and workers in large, not very well organised factories:

In a factory of, say, two thousand workers (pupils), a hundred charge hands (teachers), twenty foremen (senior staff) and two or three directors (head and deputies) it would be astonishing to find a workforce that would accept a system in which each worker was engaged on seven or eight different pieces of work each day, for several different charge-hands, in seven or eight different work-places to seven or eight different standards. This, effectively, is what occurs in many secondary schools... (pp. 82–3)

Variations in the informal rules of each classroom are implicit in Rabinowitz's argument. All social groups have rules to regulate the behaviour of their members. In secondary schools a few rules are explicit, for example not leaving the school without permission in the lunch hour, wearing the correct uniform in more or less the approved way, not smoking anywhere on school premises and so on. However, schools that seek to regulate too much of their behaviour by means of a formal set of rules encounter three problems. First, the more rules a school has, the more opportunities pupils have to break them. Secondly, externally defined codes of conduct tend to reduce pupils', and teachers', motivation to think about the reasons for their behaviour. Thirdly, no set of formal rules can ever hope to encompass the range of informal rules that exist in every classroom.

As we argued in Chapters 4 and 6, teachers naturally expect pupils to accept the rules they consider necessary for the safe and efficient running of their class. These rules vary depending on the teacher's own temperament and preferred teaching methods, the nature of the subject, and the requirements of a particular task. In these respects teachers are no different from leaders of any other social group. When pupils do not conform to the normal expectations of the classroom, they invoke sanctions – again like leaders of any other social group. These may include talking to the pupil privately, firmly drawing public attention to the problems he or she is causing, making the pupil sit in a different place, or referring the problem to the head of department or head of year. In their turn, these colleagues may see the pupil individually, impose a detention or discuss the matter with the pupil's parents. In broad terms, acceptance of a teacher's general expectations is seen as 'normal'. Children who continue to present serious behavioural problems may be seen as needing special 'help'. The same, incidentally, applies to children who fail to make the expected progress in the curriculum. A high proportion of children seen by educational psychologists are referred on account of behaviour problems, often in conjunction with learning difficulties.

This, too, raises questions about psychology's contribution to secondary teaching. Psychologists can draw on research evidence on the 'normality' of different behaviour in purely statistical terms. Thus, they can tell parents the percentage of children that are left-handed, and reassure them that this carries no implications for future educational problems. Similarly, they can reassure teachers that shy or withdrawn children are likely to improve, whereas other problems such as truancy, stealing or bullying are more likely to persist. Unreassuringly, an honest psychologist would have to add that both statements remain true irrespective of whether specialised help is provided. Ultimately, however, psychologists have to make a value judgement on the significance of behaviour problems referred to them. This should entail considering the problem from the teacher's point of view as well as its relevance to the child's current and future development. Hence teachers have a legitimate expectation that psychologists should be able to help them with problems of classroom management.

Few educational psychologists would quarrel with this expectation.

They claim expertise in methods of behaviour change that have particular relevance to teachers. Yet behind the teacher's decision to seek specialised help, and the psychologist's acceptance of the referral, lie assumptions about 'normal' personal and social development and 'normal' discipline. Thirty years ago many schools required pupils to stand in silence when a visitor entered the classroom. Today that is blessedly rare except in the most formal independent schools. What constitutes 'normal' behaviour and 'normal' discipline changes with popular and professional opinion. As important, different tasks in school demand different styles of behaviour (see Chapter 4). The methods that teachers and psychologists use to help/encourage, coerce children into acceptable behaviour also change. Thanks to the European Court of Human Rights, corporal punishment has finally been abolished in Britain. Similarly, some of the more extreme methods of behaviour modification, such as placing children in 'time-out' isolation rooms, have been quietly dropped. What remains constant is the link between the teacher's need for discipline and control on the one hand and assumptions about pupils' personal and social development on the other.

Classroom management and children's moral development

The need for rules is logically independent of the need for children to understand the reasons for them. Toddlers, for example, are taught not to put their fingers into electric plug sockets without having any clear understanding of the precise reasons. Similarly, some teachers who are noted for their limited attention to detail in their own dress see nothing illogical in punishing pupils for not wearing the correct uniform: this implies that rules must be obeyed because they *are* rules, not because they are logical or necessary. Yet if we are committed to enable pupils to develop as active learners it is important that they should understand reasons for what teachers and parents expect of them, and recognise the consequences of not conforming to these expectations. If, then, we see children as actively involved in their own learning we cannot sensibly set standards of behaviour without reference to what they understand by right and wrong. Kohlberg (1975) has argued that this is related to their level of cognitive development. He proposed six stages of moral development (see Table 7.1) but suggested that many people never progress beyond stage 4. Kohlberg's higher stages of moral reasoning imply the moral right to question the prevailing norms in a society, as reflected, for example, in national legislation or in school rules. Thus, rules can, and sometimes should, be challenged.

Kohlberg's theory has been widely criticised, not least because there is no necessary relationship between moral reasoning ability and actual behaviour. Nevertheless, it raises an interesting question about teachers' responses to 'difficult' behaviour. To what level of moral reasoning do the most frequently used responses appeal? Some schools make the sanctions for breaking specific rules explicit, perhaps involving a 'tariff' system: if you don't do your homework you get a detention, but if you swear at a teacher you get excluded. The most extreme form of this approach is seen in some American schools, which have developed elaborate discipline codes specifying the sanctions to be applied on the first occasion of each offence and on subsequent offences.[4]

Table 7.1 **Kohlberg's theory of moral reasoning**

Level 1 'Pre-conventional': corresponds to Piaget's pre-operational stage: approximate age 2–7

> *Stage 1*:   Obedience/conformity due solely to fear of punishment. *Example*: You mustn't talk when the teacher tells you to be quiet because you might get told off.
> *Stage 2*:   Morality based on 'fair trades'. *Example*: You must share your toys with other children so that they will share theirs with you.

Level 2 'Conventional': corresponds to Piaget's (1965) 'moral realism': approximate age 7–11

> *Stage 3*:   Judgement based on desire to please others. *Example*: It's wrong to swear because it upsets mum (teacher).
> *Stage 4*:   Judgement based on respect for authority, maintaining law and order. *Example*: You mustn't break rules even if you don't agree with them. What would happen if everyone decided on rules for themselves?

Level 3 'Post-conventional': corresponds to Piaget's (1965) 'moral relativism':

> *Stage 5*:   Rules can be changed if there is general agreement. *Example*: Why is this rule really necessary?
> *Stage 6*:   Respect for human dignity: abstract principles can transcend rules. *Example*: I won't obey this rule because it's against my principles.

In Britain most teachers prefer to retain some flexibility in their use of sanctions. Thus detention may not *always* be used for a particular offence, though it may be the most usual response. This indicates another limitation in Kohlberg's theory. A strict tariff system appears to be appealing unambiguously to stage 1. This is evident in the discipline systems of some secondary schools but is developmentally appropriate to pre-school children. Often, though, teachers use this after trying other approaches. In talking to pupils individually they may succeed in appealing to their understanding of the consequences if no one accepted a rule: What will happen if we get more complaints from local shop-keepers about behaviour during the lunch hour? Or:

Do *you* think you will get the GCSE grades you need if you continue to do so little homework?

These appeals are essentially to stages 3 and 4 on Kohlberg's scheme. The superficial fairness of specific punishments for specific offences conceals the fact that pupils can behave in the same or similar ways for widely different reasons. Moreover, if we treat adolescents in a way that is cognitively more appropriate to pre-school children we must not be surprised if they fail to 'learn' to behave responsibly in the absence of external restraints. In universities it is often easy to spot students from public schools and formal grammar schools: without the pressures of tightly organised academic and discipline systems, many of them go through a belated stage of adolescent rebellion. Tariff systems of punishment can sometimes have a deterrent effect, provided the connection between the act and the response is immediate. Yet from the point of view of personal and social development they are at best useless. They do little to develop respect for the moral legitimacy of rules, nor, incidentally, do they give teachers any incentive for questioning the necessity for a rule. Rather they encourage deviousness by instilling respect for the eleventh commandment: 'Thou shalt not be found out.'

Personal and social education and the curriculum

Both the official, or National Curriculum, and the hidden curriculum contribute to children's personal and social education. The hidden curriculum can be defined as the network of relations in a school – between teachers, between pupils and between teachers and pupils – which determine what teachers and pupils expect of themselves and of each other. Both pupils' and teachers' expectations are influenced by the structure of the society in which they live. Authors with a Marxist orientation tend to regard the social and economic divisions in society as having an overwhelming influence on the hidden curriculum (e.g. Bowles and Gintis, 1976). This deterministic view underestimates the ability both of teachers and pupils to take independent action in protection of their interests.[5] Nevertheless, it is difficult to underestimate the importance of the hidden curriculum. It includes all incidental learning and reflects the social and emotional climate of the school. Many sociologists see it as one of the most powerful means by which society defines the value attached to different kinds and levels of achievement, and thereby shapes the future behaviour of its citizens.

The National Curriculum may contain messages that are transmitted through the hidden curriculum. Thus, more time is allocated to Maths than to Music, to Science than to Physical Education. Additional influences in the hidden curriculum lie in the organisation of the class, the school and the education system itself. We have already referred to the 'lessons' children learn about sex roles from the organisation of classes. Relationships between senior and main professional grade staff are a further influence. The existence of the private sector draws explicit attention to the power of money to buy what many parents see as educational privilege. For parents and for children it is a short step from believing that education at the local secondary school is unsatisfactory to concluding that the children who attend it are less desirable as friends. City technology colleges and grant-maintained schools may produce the same divisiveness within the state system as already exists between state and independent schools.

Personal and social education does not form part of the National Curriculum. On the other hand, teachers' conditions of service explicitly require them to communicate and consult with parents and outside bodies, take part in meetings about pastoral arrangements and promote 'the general progress and well-being of individual pupils and of any class or group of pupils' assigned to them (DES, 1988a, p. 23). In addition the National Curriculum Council has argued publicly that personal and social education should be seen as one of a number of cross-curricular themes (NCC, 1989b).

The status of personal and social education in the secondary curriculum is, in fact, highly problematic. It is not a legally required subject in the National Curriculum, yet many schools contain a timetabled slot for 'PSE'. Both the content and methods vary widely (DES, 1988e) and it is seldom clear how the timetabled PSE course complements the other influences on pupils' personal and social development from the official and hidden curriculum. If we accept that some of the most powerful influences on young people's personal and social development are transmitted through the hidden curriculum, it is nonsensical to argue that personal and social education can be confined to a small timetabled slot in the official or National Curriculum. Theoretically, it would be nice to think that *everything* that happens in schools, both through the National Curriculum and through the hidden National Curriculum contributes beneficially to pupils' personal and social development. Regrettably, we have not yet reached this happy state of affairs. Regarding the whole area as unproblematic prevents a clear analysis of ways in which schools affect their pupils' personal and social development.

Some background considerations

Two aspects of secondary education present particular difficulty in planning a programme for personal and social education. The first is the subject-based nature of secondary education. The second is the development of pastoral care networks in which the heads of year or house enjoy similar status to heads of subject departments. The subject divisions are self-evident. All teaching has implications for pupils' personal and social development, but in some subjects they are more immediate than in others. It is difficult, for example, to imagine teaching English Literature without explicit discussion of relationships between people, or to imagine PE teaching without reference to health education and to pupils' awareness of individual differences in physical coordination. Planning a curriculum which, by definition, crosses subject boundaries, presents the obvious problems that teachers will vary widely both in their understanding of personal and social education and in the importance they attach to it. Some heads of department encourage their colleagues to teach in a way that encourages social awareness. Others consider themselves bound by the letter of the curriculum and see no need to step outside it. To take one example, the concepts of science and of computer technology are morally neutral. Science can be used for the benefit or the destruction of humankind. Computers can be used to guide missiles in the final world war or to provide a more fulfilling life for disabled people. An imaginative teacher can introduce science or technology in a way that extends children's understanding of its practical application and potential benefits. Given the popularity of 'space invaders' and similar computer war games which implicitly equate the use of computers with aggression, this appears particularly desirable.

Problems arising from variation between teachers in their understanding of personal and social education can be compounded by the way a school organises its pastoral care network. This is by no means inevitable. We do, however, need to recognise some of the practical and theoretical problems in pastoral care.

Pastoral care or social control?

In the selective system of education, heads and deputy heads of grammar and secondary modern schools undertook responsibility for pupils' welfare. As long as schools remained small this was perhaps manageable, but with the introduction of much larger comprehensive schools it was no longer credible. It became apparent that a formal structure was needed to cater for pupil welfare. Pastoral care may not have been invented by comprehensive schools, but they were certainly responsible for placing it on an institutional footing. Head teachers and governors started to appoint heads of year or house, and a career ladder was created in parallel to the ladder leading to headship of a subject department.

Why and how this happened is a matter for debate. The conventional wisdom of pastoral care holds that its origins reflect the influence of the public school system with its emphasis on character training (e.g. Best *et al.*, 1980). This may be an over-simplification. It is cynical but not unrealistic to point out that posts of responsibility for pastoral care provided 'consolation prizes' for heads of department in former secondary modern schools when their former grammar school equivalent was appointed head of department in the new comprehensive. Today, pastoral care continues to provide an alternative career ladder for teachers who are unable, or do not wish, to obtain promotion as head of a subject department.

Yet this was probably not the main factor in the growth of pastoral care networks. Comprehensive schools, by definition, required teachers to cater for a much wider ability range than the previous selective system. Teaching, in other words, was becoming more difficult, and teachers felt that behaviour problems were increasing. It is doubtful whether this was in fact the case since the evidence from the 1920s and 1930s suggests that behaviour problems then were at least as prevalent and as severe as they are now (Galloway *et al.*, 1982). On the other hand, parents were probably expecting more from the education system by the 1970s and teachers were certainly more aware of the needs of their less able and less cooperative pupils. The 1969 Children's and Young Persons Act was creating, or perhaps reflecting, a climate which regarded problem behaviour as a symptom of personal or family disadvantage. At the same time professional and public opinion was becoming increasingly critical of sanctions such as corporal punishment, which had seldom previously been questioned. Pastoral care networks, then, could easily be seen as a response to the new comprehensive school's need for control in the increasingly liberal climate of the 1960s and 1970s.

However, this analysis presents both theoretical and practical problems. The theory, or perhaps simply the rhetoric, of pastoral care emphasised its function in the school as a caring community. The reality, as Best *et al.* (1983) demonstrate in their detailed study of pastoral care in one school, was concerned with matters of organisation such as lunch-time passes, supervision of bus queues, and behaviour. In many schools, pastoral care came to be equated with penal care, since heads of year were routinely responsible for investigating and dealing with cases of disruptive behaviour. Experience on INSET courses for pastoral heads shows that this is a continuing pattern.

It does, however, raise two problems. First, the belief that disruptive behaviour can be 'cured' by counselling from a head of year, or from anyone else, is naive and unsupported by evidence. Indeed, the evidence from studies of the effectiveness of counselling and psychotherapy suggests that disruptive pupils are much less likely than most other pupils with problems to benefit from this form of intervention (e.g. Levitt, 1963; Mitchell and Rosa, 1981). The second problem is more pragmatic. Giving heads of year responsibility for investigating and dealing with problem behaviour surrounded the role of other teachers in ambiguity. Subject teachers were nominally responsible for discipline in their classroooms, yet a colleague at 'middle management' level also had that responsibility. Teachers who might have hesitated to refer a problem, such as chewing gum in class, to the head teacher for fear of appearing ridiculous had much less compunction in passing it over to a less senior colleague who might lack the confidence or the status to tell them to sort it out themselves.

The role of the form tutor was surrounded in even greater ambiguity. One function of the pastoral network was to ensure that every pupil had a point of contact with at least one teacher. It was unrealistic to expect a head of year to know all pupils in the year-group well; there might be as many as 300 in a large school. Consequently, the form tutor would be the basic unit of pastoral care. Because pupils might be taught by as many as ten teachers in the course of a week, and because each subject teacher might see as many as 500 pupils during the week, the form tutor was the only practical person to whom responsibility for getting to know a small group of pupils well could be delegated. Unfortunately, while theoretically this was recognised, its practical implications were not.

In discussing research projects in fourteen secondary schools in Sheffield (UK) and in New Zealand, Galloway (1983) noted that all head teachers acknowledged form tutors as providing the basis for pastoral care; yet the organisation of pastoral care in many of these schools made their role virtually impossible. This could happen: (a) because they changed tutor groups each year thus making continuity of care difficult; (b) they only saw their tutor groups for 10 minutes each day and consequently felt that their main responsibility as form tutors was the low-grade clerical chore of completing the register; (c) they did not teach their subject specialism to pupils in their tutor group, and therefore lacked the opportunity this might have given to get to know the pupils in a different context; (d) the year tutor's job was defined in terms of investigating and dealing with problems, with the result that form tutors felt that pastoral care was their responsibility, and the form tutor's role was to refer problems to them.

This rather depressing scenario was not evident in all schools. Indeed, it was at least in part as a result of growing recognition of problems in the concept and practice of pastoral care that academics and practitioners started to develop tutorial activities that might give the form tutor a more constructive role within the pastoral care network (e.g. Button, 1981; Baldwin and Wells, 1979). These programmes, while perhaps useful and important in themselves, are limited by their focus on the work of form tutors. Personal and social education has much wider implications for the curriculum and for the social climate of the school. Although this was never the authors' intention, a programme for form tutors could all too easily equate personal and social education with tutorial work, thus reducing it to a marginal activity and confirming a spurious distinction between the academic curriculum and pastoral activities.

There is something more than faintly futile about a form tutor's use of activities designed to develop trusting relationships (for example, a blindfolded pupil being guided round the room by another pupil) in a school in which trusting relationships are conspicuously lacking. The futility lies not in the activity itself, but in the simplistic view that an activity which is inconsistent with everthing else that is happening in a school can compensate for its shortcomings. One does not have to be an experimental psychologist to recognise problems of learning transfer and to know that skills acquired in one context, whether academic or social, are unlikely to generalise to other contexts unless opportunities are provided for practising them.

If this analysis is correct, it follows that tutorial work should build on and extend the best of the social and educational learning that takes place in the rest of the school. In schools that have developed trusting relationships and in which effort is valued as highly as achievement, many of the more personally challenging activities in tutorial programmes will be both appropriate and useful. This is not, however, always the case. The question, then, is how to plan a curriculum for personal and social development that recognises the importance not only of form tutors, but also of the mainstream curriculum.

Two stages in curriculum development

In their study of twelve London comprehensive schools, Rutter *et al.* (1979) noted a tendency in the more successful schools for heads of department to involve their colleagues in planning the curriculum. In these schools, teachers did not have complete autonomy over what they taught, since curriculum planning was a joint responsibility. This also has implications for planning the school's programme for personal and social education.

An outline programme for each year-group is needed. The hierarchical structure of secondary schools, together with the way pastoral care is organised, suggests that a deputy head might convene and chair a working group consisting of the five heads of year. The group would have two tasks. First, they would need to focus on the programme's content. This will vary from school to school, but there are core issues that will require attention. These include: (a) careers education and pupils' understanding of the world of work, health and sex education; (b) study skills and their ability to make effective use of resources available in the school; (c) awareness of their rights and responsibilities in the local community and in the wider society; and (d) relationships within the school and outside it. The programme will need to ensure that the major areas contributing to personal and social education are covered, and that there is an age-appropriate development from year to year. This constitutes the basis for a curriculum for personal and social education.

The next stage is perhaps more difficult and involves translating the curriculum into a programme: Who will be responsible in each year-group for each area of the curriculum? Clearly, certain subject departments are likely to make a major contribution, for example Biology, Home Economics and PE in health education. Planning is needed, though, to ensure that the school does not restrict access to parts of the curriculum to a minority of pupils. Planning is also needed to avoid duplication, for example, pupils being shown the same sex education film twice in one week (a complaint a pupil once made when I asked him why teachers were complaining about his behaviour).

The extent to which each subject department contributes to the personal and social education programme will depend on its priorities. Thus, the Geography curriculum is likely at some stage to include study of aspects of the local community. How far this can extend to analysis of social issues will vary from department to department, depending both on the teachers' skills in discussing potentially contentious issues with children and on the way they view their subject.

As well as identifying areas of the programme that would best be covered in subject departments, the planning team will need to consider how to make best use of specific expertise within the school. It seems wasteful, for example, for a careers specialist to spend a lot of time with each third-year class providing basic information about the option system that could perfectly well have been provided by form tutors.

A further point is that some areas within a personal and social education programme may be thought to require specialised teaching. The planning team may recognise that the expertise of particular teachers would best be used in addressing issues with which many other teachers would feel uncomfortable. Matters of personal and sexual morality are an obvious example. Hence, there may be a case for a PSE course that would be seen as forming part of an overall programme.

The tutorial programme will now consist of those aspects of the personal and social education programme that are not to be covered in subject departments nor in a PSE course. This does not imply negative criteria for identifying issues for the tutorial programme. In considering aspects that can be covered by subject departments, the planning team will need to balance the time available for tutorial work against an assessment as to whether a particular tutorial team, for example first-year form tutors, could handle a topic more or less effectively than a particular subject department, e.g. Geography or Home Economics.

Thus, the planning team provides an outline programme for each year-group. The tutors in each year group form the tutorial team, coordinated by the head of year. Their task is to translate the tutorial programme into a syllabus, specifying in greater detail the topics that will be tackled at different stages throughout the year.

One way to tackle this is to divide the year's programme into a number of themes, and allocate each theme a proportion of the total number of tutorial periods. This will vary from school to school, but most schools timetable between one and three form sessions within each theme. Activities from published tutorial programmes may be useful. Schools Television produces a wide range of programmes that can be invaluable in tutorial work. They include *Tutorial Topics, Scene*, and series on anti-racism, study skills, careers guidance and health education. For some themes visiting speakers may be appropriate.

Dividing the year's programme into themes and deciding how many sessions to allocate to each theme is an activity for the whole tutorial team, though not necessarily a lengthy one. Planning sessions within a theme need involve no more than one or two tutors, with back-up support from the head of year. Thus, if two tutors undertake to plan four sessions for a theme on use of leisure, they will produce an outline for each session, with suggested activities. These will then be duplicated for use by the other form tutors. Few subject teachers will want, or be able, to plan all tutorial sessions themselves. They should, however, be able to produce plans for two or three a term. Circulating these for use by colleagues develops a sense of accountability within the team, since no one will want a reputation for producing inadequate or boring material. If every member of the tutorial team accepts responsibility for producing plans for two or three sessions a term, excessive demands are made on no one, but everyone makes a significant contribution to the programme.

Clearly, this model calls for a high level of coordinating ability from the head of year. It also requires the head of year to be well informed about resources on which individual or pairs of tutors may draw when planning their sessions. It does not, however, require the heads of year to do all the work themselves. Indeed, if the tutorial team is to function effectively it is essential that every member should not only contribute to the programme, but be seen to be contributing. In other words, the head of year's task is to create an ethos in the tutorial team in which teachers regard tutorial activities as an important part of their work.

All this raises questions about assessment. Superficially, this can be carried out by monitoring the knowledge, skills, attitudes and concepts which children acquire or develop from their school's personal and social education programme. Yet assessment of children's personal and social development has to go much further than this, requiring a broader picture of their overall development. That, however, is only possible in terms of the school's aims for its pupils' personal and social development. This brings us back to the qualities that teachers, parents, school governors, the LEA and central government believe children should be developing at school. To say these are essentially political value judgements, and therefore not part of a teacher's job, is an evasion of responsibility. The fact that a school is part of a wider community does not mean teachers can avoid making a statement of their own position on basic moral issues. A community with no values is an amoral one. If we are clear about the moral and social aims of schooling, we shall wish to develop ways of monitoring pupils' development that extend beyond their progress in subjects of the National Curriculum (see Chapter 8).

Personal and social education and parents

Teachers vary widely in their beliefs and values. Indeed, the sheer variety of their beliefs and values is one of the most powerful arguments for developing an agreed policy on the values the school seeks to develop in pupils. Parents are likely to differ even more widely, if only because there are more of them. Successive Education Acts have shifted the balance of power between teachers and parents in the latter's favour. The 1980 Act required secondary schools to publish public examination results. It also required the publication of HMI reports on schools, gave parents access to greater information about a school's organisation and curriculum, and extended their rights to choose their child's school. The 1981 Act gave parents extensive rights to involvement in the assessment of their child's special educational needs, including copies of professional reports. The 1986 Act ensured their representation on all governing bodies. The 1988 Act gave them the National Curriculum, the promise of information on their children's performance in the proposed national testing programme, the possibility of opting out of LEA control by seeking grant-maintained status, and a further increase in choice of their child's school.

There is little doubt that the motivation behind all this legislation was the government's view that schools had been insufficiently responsive to parents' aspirations and unreasonably secretive both in their control of the curriculum and in their communication with parents. Nor is there much doubt that schools in Britain compare unfavourably with those in other EC countries in terms of the quality of cooperation between home and school (Macbeth, 1984). A deeply entrenched part of staff-room folklore in many schools – especially those serving council housing estates, inner-city areas and areas with many pupils from minority ethnic communities – is that parental 'apathy' is widespread.

The evidence does not support this view. Numerous studies of parental interest in their children's education have demonstrated that parents are much more actively interested than is accepted by the conventional wisdom in many staff rooms (e.g. Johnson and Ransom, 1983). In addition, a one-sidedness is evident in a lot of 'liaison' with parents. Teachers often see their task as educating parents about the school rather than as understanding the parents' own values and priorities. Cooperative parents, then, are ones who do not rock the boat, content to support the school even when a more objective view might suggest that their child's curricular or social needs are not adequately being met.

Making schools parent friendly

How much the individual form tutor or head of year can do to foster an effective partnership with parents will depend to some extent on the school's senior management. They can make the school 'parent friendly', or provide hidden messages that deter parents even more effectively than a circular letter asking them to confine their visits to the termly open evening except in emergencies. In this section we consider how schools can develop effective links with parents.

While it is clear that almost all secondary schools can point to a wide variety of formal and less formal contacts with parents (Woods, 1984) it is equally clear (a) that teachers often complain that the parents they least often see are the ones they most need to see, and (b) that schools vary widely in their success in encouraging parents to take an active and collaborative interest in their children's education. It is not too difficult to see why some secondary schools have limited success in this respect. For some parents, the termly open evening involves listening to one teacher after another provide an embarrassing catalogue of their child's shortcomings. If the problem is one of behaviour as well as progress they may feel they are expected to effect change by remote control: 'Will you please do something about your son's behaviour when I'm in charge of him, but without coming anywhere near the classroom in which I'm teaching him?' The words will be different, but the message clear enough.

Yet the picture need not be this bleak. Social events such as plays and concerts and fund-raising activities are often well attended. They provide a useful shop window for the school, but their value in persuading parents to take an interest in their children's day-to-day work in the classroom is doubtful. There is a lack of systematic research in secondary schools, but evidence from junior schools has suggested that schools with an active Parent–Teacher Association are not more likely than other schools to demonstrate effectiveness on criteria such as pupils' behaviour and educational progress. In contrast, effectiveness does seem to be associated with the quality of informal links on pupil-centred matters (Mortimore *et al.,* 1988).

A study of home–school links in secondary schools in Wales showed that 79 per cent of parents at one school, most of them in working-class jobs, had read the newsletter or magazine, compared with 2 per cent at another (Woods, 1984). Perhaps not surprisingly, 90 per cent of parents at the former were satisfied with the arrangements for involving parents, compared with an average of 78 per cent at all other schools. More surprising was the observation that *more* parents at this school expressed some concern regarding their child's education than at any other school in the survey. The implication was that success in persuading parents to take an active interest in their children's secondary education could lead them to become more concerned about aspects of their progress rather than less.

Yet perhaps this was neither surprising nor discouraging. A successful partnership between home and school does not imply that parents are socialised into providing uncritical support for everything the school does. Rather it implies that parents make full use of all the available information to monitor their children's progress. To expect parents to take an active but uncritical interest is almost a contradiction in terms.

Teachers' conditions of service require them to be available to discuss children's work with parents. Annual or termly parents' evenings remain the most frequent way of meeting this requirement but are not always satisfactory for either party. More frequent and less formal contacts generally provide more effective communication. This can be achieved in many ways, of which three provide examples. First, homework diaries provide a potentially effective way of keeping parents and teachers in touch with each other. They are unlikely to be much use, though, if parents are asked to do no more than sign the 'diary' at the end of each week. Woods (1984) noted that some schools asked parents for comments and observations and provided space for this. Space for teacher's replies is, of course, equally important. Galloway (1985a) noted one head teacher's view that this facilitated communication by removing the need for formal typed letters that might intimidate some parents.

Secondly, research in primary schools has suggested how parents may work with teachers in helping children with reading difficulties. Tizard *et al.* (1982) showed that children whose parents listened to them read from work they had brought home from school made better progress than children receiving extra reading lessons at school from an experienced teacher. Parents were *not* given elaborate guidance on *how* to listen to their children. As important, the research took place in Haringey, a socially disadvantaged part of London. Haringey was precisely the sort of area in which parents, according to conventional wisdom, were least likely to be able or willing to help in their children's education. The greater complexity of the secondary curriculum will prevent schools extending this approach on a large scale, but the head of one large secondary school reported (in a personal communication) that it was playing an effective part in his colleagues' work with backward readers.

Finally, in most cases a climate of trust and confidence can be achieved when parents visit the school. There are, however, occasions when parents cannot visit the school, either because they are working or because they are suffering from poor health. There are also occasions when teachers may feel that a child's welfare requires a closer understanding of the child's problems than is possible in the more formal setting of the school. In such circumstances a home visit can be useful. Home visiting is not something that all teachers find easy. Visiting with a more experienced colleague can be helpful on the first few occasions.

Marland (1985, p. 106) lists four advantages in discussing a child's welfare in her or his own home. They are:

1. The school's representative has demonstrated sufficient concern to visit, and this fact alone is encouraging to parents or guardians.
2. The pupil's parents or guardians are on *their* home ground, offering *their* hospitality, and this often gives them an added confidence and willingness to share.
3. In the home, the centrality of the pupil is symbolically more obvious and powerful than in school, where convenience of the school's system can loom larger.
4. Only in the pupil's own home setting is it possible to really learn about his or her background sympathetically, and to learn from parents or guardians.

Conclusions

We have argued that schools have an inevitable impact on their pupils' personal and social development simply because pupils attend them. The impact may not be in the desired direction. In a devastating attack on much contemporary comprehensive schooling Hargreaves (1982, p. 17) claims that the secondary school system exerts on many pupils: 'a destruction of their dignity which is so massive and so pervasive that few subsequently recover from it'.

The principal victims, he claims, are working-class children. Hargreaves is perhaps uncritical of primary teachers since there is evidence that the ability of working-class children is frequently underestimated by teachers in nursery schools (Tizard and Hughes, 1984) and in infant schools (Tizard *et al.*, 1988). The origins of the low self-esteem and chronic under-achievement which Hargreaves identifies in secondary schools are evident many years earlier. On the other hand, HMI have repeatedly criticised what they see as unnecessarily low expectations of secondary pupils, particularly in working-class areas and in low-ability groups. Both the main political parties share this view of the under-achievement of a large minority of secondary pupils. Schooling, then, is widely seen as damaging to the self-esteem of many pupils.

Yet teachers unquestionably aim to raise children's self-esteem. They seek to do this by enhancing their feelings of personal involvement in classroom activities, as well as by giving them recognition as individual members of a class. Against these liberal aims stand the teacher's need for control and society's expectations with respect both to children's behaviour and to their educational progress. This is perhaps the major dilemma of contemporary schooling. The social interactionist view of learning that we have advocated in Chapters 4–6 may not solve this dilemma but we believe it goes some way towards doing so.

In other words, we should be cautiously optimistic. The principal theme of this chapter is that schools can contribute in constructive ways to their pupils' personal and social development. Yet the fact that they will inevitably have an effect shows why education is, and will remain a topic of interest to politicians as well as to psychologists. Bluntly, politicians may well be interested in the skills and knowledge that are taught through the National Curriculum but they will be much more interested, irrespective of party, in the values and attitudes that schools develop in their pupils. In other words their principal interest is in pupils' personal and social development.

In a democracy it is, of course, wholly inappropriate for teachers and school governors to follow blindly the biases and prejudices of the party in power. This would be as unreasonable as basing everything that happens in education on one particular school of psychological thought. Nevertheless, there is now a solid body of research to support the political pressure for teachers to establish closer and more effective partnerships with their pupils' parents. Equally, our knowledge of the way children learn suggests that they adapt rapidly and apparently effortlessly to different situations. Personal and social education is bound up with notions of behaviour, attitudes and values. These cannot be compartmentalised. They develop from children's overall experience in the family, the school and elsewhere. For teachers this implies that personal and social education should be regarded as an integral part of the curriculum. To do so requires a policy for the whole school as well as for each class. The demands on teachers are considerable, but this is central to children's experience at school.

Notes and further reading

1. For further reading in personal and social education see: Hargreaves *et al.* (1988); Pring (1984); and Ryder and Campbell (1988).
2. The essential point here is that children, like adults, attribute causes to their experiences of success or failure. The nature of their attributions affects their subsequent motivation to attempt a task. See Weiner (1979) and (1984).
3. This perspective on the origins of universal compulsory education is described in greater detail by Rubinstein (1969).
4. For examples of discipline codes in US schools, see Safer (1987).
5. David Hargreaves (1982) provides a lively discussion of ways in which pupils and teachers protect their own interests.

Seminar suggestions

1. Make a detailed record of the activities of one pupil, or of a small group of pupils in the course of one lesson or activity (e.g. assembly). As far as possible, record everything the children do *and* the instructions they receive from their teacher, the questions they are asked, etc. In the seminar examine these records and consider what the children may be learning through the hidden curriculum. What effects is this learning likely to have on their personal and social development?
2. Describe a child you regard as having a reputation with other pupils for 'difficult' behaviour. How far is this behaviour maintained by the pupil's status in his/her peer group? As a teacher, how can you set about changing this?
3. Plan a health education programme for one year-group, integrating it with the work the pupils will be following in other curriculum areas, e.g. Biology, Home Economics, PE, RE. Indicate how the content of this programme will 'mesh' with that of the previous year-group and the following one.

CHAPTER 8

Assessment and evaluation

The relationship between assessment and evaluation

Both the assessment of pupil performance and the evaluation of
teacher action are central to the models of interactive pedagogy we
have been discussing. The assessment of pupils' performance on task
is essential to the planning of future learning experiences. While
frequently referred to as informal classroom assessment, this process
serves two useful purposes. It may be diagnostic, in the sense that it
can reveal to the teacher/assessor strengths and weaknesses in a
learner's understanding or mastery of concepts or skills. It is also
formative, both in the sense that it focuses on the acquisition of skills
and concepts and in the way that it is consequently used to inform
teacher decision making in task setting. The assessment of pupils is
therefore an integral element in the evaluation processes employed by
teachers when reviewing their own pedagogical practices.

Assessment of pupils and evaluation of the curriculum can go hand
in hand. In Chapters 5 and 6 we outlined a learning process that occurs
in classrooms in which the teacher has to note the learner's progress
through a series of learning experiences in order to know when to
move the pupil on to the next stage in the cycle, from introduction of
skills and information to constructing an understanding and finally to
practice. Finally, judgements on mastery are made when children are
engaged in more routine practice activities. At the same time as
assessing performance on tasks, teachers evaluate the tasks themselves.
They query whether the activities are actually providing children with
the intended learning experiences and whether the appropriate amount
of instruction has been given at the right time and pace. Continuous,
formative assessment, supported by evaluations of pedagogy,
therefore, underpin good practice.

Assessment and evaluation in the 1990s

These two issues both dominate and are dominated by the
implementation of a national curriculum.[1] The introduction of a
nationally applied set of curriculum guidelines that are sustained by a
hierarchically organised set of expected levels of pupil attainment

suggests a particular form of assessment in secondary schools. An important and related evaluation issue also arises. The latter was best summarised by Holt (1987) when he criticised the 'mechanistic assumption that schools can be run like biscuit factories'. Holt objected to the simplistic view of evaluation that is encouraged by such a clearly defined national curriculum, as this is based on the belief that if schools are provided with equipment and targets, appropriate products will emerge. An alarming consequence of such a view of evaluation is that performance of pupils against nationally prescribed targets can provide the sole basis for judging schools. Here assessment and evaluation are closely linked, but not necessarily with the processes of pupil learning in mind.

Assessment

A Martian on a flying visit to Britain in the latter part of the 1980s may well have been excused the opinion that the introduction of a national curriculum was in fact the introduction of a national system of assessment. In 1985, *Better Schools* set the tone with: 'The Government's central aim is to improve standards in schools, using the available resources to yield the best possible returns' (DES, 1985, p. 90). Clearly mindful of the view that the assessment system drives the task system, the assessment tail was set in motion to wag the curriculum dog.

An example of the rigidity deemed necessary to ensure curriculum uniformity was the organisation of levels of pupil attainment into specific linear hierarchies of progression. The simple linear model for attainment targets was not the only option available. Noss *et al.* (1989) observed that it might have been preferable to have mapped out a range of possible routes for the learner. However, the prescribed pathway through the curriculum has been clearly way-marked by assessible criteria of performance at specific levels on each attainment target.

The result at classroom level is that teachers are faced not only with a clearly defined body of knowledge and skills into which pupils should be inducted, but also a clearly delineated order of acquisition, which may not, in reality, match the order in which children do make sense of events (see Driver (1983) on children's acquisition of scientific knowledge).

The importance of the way-marks, in the form of levels of attainment, may present the greatest obstacle to the success of a national curriculum. Performance-based criteria ensure that a curriculum is reduced to a minimal set of learning objectives and that considerable teacher time is given to rigorous assessment at these significant points. Broadfoot (1988) looks to the experience of the

United States in this area and notes the lack of relationship between improvements in test scores and an emphasis on testing. Indeed, the United States experience suggests that time involved in testing and the high drop-out rate of weaker students has resulted in a move towards an appreciation of teacher professionalism and away from control through testing. The control issue, implicit in a national testing programme, is important particularly when it relates to evaluation of learning experiences.[2]

Evaluation

The evaluation systems found in schools tend to serve a variety of purposes. Bates (1984) categorised these as pedagogical, individual development, organisational development and accountability. The pedagogical level provides the basis for the curricular decision making we have already described. The role of evaluation in the development of the individual teacher and the organisation has been a feature of much educational discussion in the 1970s and 1980s (e.g. Stenhouse, 1975; Skilbeck, 1984; Simons, 1987). It now appears that the accountability aspects of evaluation may be increased by the introduction of a centrally orchestrated curriculum for all state schools.

The connection between assessment and evaluation is a complex one. Goldstein (1987 and 1988) points to the dangers of simplistic comparison of schools by results, given the general acceptance that the achievement of pupils on entry to a school is the most important predictor of later achievement. Consequently, Goldstein claims that comparisons of schools should be based on the progress made by pupils. Whether the simple outcome measure or a more subtle gauge of progress is taken as the criterion, it seems likely that institutional evaluation will necessarily have some focus on those elements of pupil performance that are highlighted by the National Curriculum.

The purposes of assessment

The use of assessment for social control is not a phenomenon unique to the 1990s. The origins of Binet's intelligence testing at the beginning of this century lie in the need to 'normalise' the educational performance of pupils. Slightly later developments in the United States used intelligence testing as the basis for sorting children into streams or 'tracks' through schooling (Chapman, 1981), while after the Second World War intelligence testing in the UK became the acceptable device for the selection of pupils for specific forms of schooling.

Intelligence testing is the prime example of normative assessment in which the concern is to gauge the performance of a child against what might normally be expected of a child of a similar age. The notion of above or below average performance results as child is compared against child, usually for purposes of selection, guidance and prediction of future performance.

Standardised tests, most commonly used for assessing reading performance, are the norm-referenced tests most familiar to teachers. Rigour in administration is crucial and administration is often time consuming. The results of the most frequently used reading tests – usually a reading age score which can be compared with the expected performance at the child's chronological age – assist in labelling the child as a good or poor reader but do nothing either to indicate causes of poor performance, for example whether they are primarily motivational or skills based, or to isolate areas of particular weakness (see Pumfrey, 1979; Vincent *et al.*, 1983). Of more assistance to teachers in their planning of programmes for pupils is the use of diagnostic techniques, for example miscue analysis (Moyle, 1979; Moon, 1984), which provide the information on strengths and weaknesses crucial to the provision of further learning experiences.

Miscue analysis in fact belongs in the category of assessment techniques also occupied by the levels of attainment prescribed by the National Curriculum assessment programme. Criterion-referenced testing, where each learner is assessed on the ability to master a particular skill or concept, is generally considered to be of more relevance to both the pupil's progress and teacher evaluation of the curriculum.

The most commonly found form of assessment in secondary school, manifesting as either the weekly test of work covered or the termly internal examination of coursework, does not, despite its intention to assess success on an element of a curriculum, always deserve to be categorised as a criterion-referenced test. While the weekly check of knowledge of formulae or dates may meet the definition, more open-ended essay questions fit less easily. Criterion-referenced testing lends itself most effectively to assessment of the 'yes, can do it' or 'no, can't do it' kind. In contrast, essay questions do not permit such a narrow range of responses. Criterion-referenced testing therefore tends to be associated with a relatively narrow mastery of skills or conceptual understanding, and a focus on the achievement of learners as they progress through a curriculum levels itself to a simple 'yes/no' response as in 'yes, can fit a mitred corner' or 'no, cannot do this'.

Nevertheless there is a considerable leap to be effected between the haphazard class test of work covered and a national system of assessment on recognised criteria of achievement which will, by necessity, allow meaningful comparison between pupils. As Nuttall and Goldstein (1986) point out, criterion-referenced assessment cannot be considered entirely independently of norm referencing. Criterion-referenced tests are constructed by collecting information on the validity of each item, that is, its ability to differentiate between the majority who can succeed on an item and those who cannot. In this way a picture of 'normal' performance is used both to suggest what might be the appropriate level of mastery of a skill on which the 'population' of pupils is assessed and in gauging the validity of that item in its ability to differentiate between competence and incompetence. Within this context norm referencing appears to strengthen criterion-referenced assessments without removing the educationally valuable information they provide for the teacher.

One obvious example of these processes at work is found within the attainment targets provided by the National Curriculum. As we have already mentioned, in terms of the National Curriculum, the relationship between curriculum, children's learning and criteria for assessment is not unproblematic, and care needs to be taken to ensure that teachers are alert to the fact that pupils' progress through curriculum areas may not always match the set linear pattern suggested by neat lists of criteria. As Harlen (1989) points out, a pupil's performance on a process skill, for example planning an investigation, will depend to some extent on the child's familiarity with the material under investigation. Similarly, we have already discussed the complex processes of constructing understanding in Chapter 5 with particular reference to the work of Watts and Bentley (1987).

While outlining the distinctions between the purposes of norm-referenced and criterion-referenced assessments we have also begun to focus on the difference between two other purposes of assessment in schools: that is, whether it is *summative* or *formative*. If assessment is essentially for the purposes of selection, long-term prediction or reporting and asks the question 'How well has the learner done?' either in comparison with others or at the end of a programme of study, the assessment is generally regarded as summative and usually enters the public domain to become available, often for reporting purposes, to parents, other colleagues, the LEA, etc. If, on the other hand, assessment is used to inform pedagogy and asks the question 'How is the learner making sense of this?' it is generally considered to be formative in nature, providing vital feedback on pupil strengths and weaknesses, and is usually initially private, remaining the direct concern of the teacher, who responds to this information with appropriate experiences for the pupil.

Formative assessment is not necessarily diagnostic, as diagnostic assessment may require the teacher to delve more deeply into a pupil's misconceptions (see Bennett *et al.*, 1984), but diagnostic assessment is certainly formative. The Task Group on Assessment and Testing (TGAT) suggest that the boundary between formative and diagnostic purposes is not sharp or clear (DES, 1988d, para. 27) but that while diagnostic assessment may sometimes be necessary, it leads to more information that may usefully be passed on to another teacher (DES,

1988d, para. 27). Nevertheless, formative and diagnostic assessments do gather vital information on the progress of children through a curriculum programme and therefore eventually need to be collated into a form that will be relatively quick to read and eventually make sense to other colleagues, particularly to the teacher of the next year-group, and so facilitate continuity in the pupil's learning from year to year.

Formative assessment, then, provides useful information at summative stages. Clearly, however, summative assessment is not produced through the simple accumulation of formative assessments. The concern of summative assessment is mainly to report what the child is capable of doing at a certain point in his or her school life and particularly to provide relevant information for employers or educators at the next stage.

Record keeping

Record-keeping systems therefore need to provide a bridge between curricular demands and children's learning in ways which both immediately assist teachers' task setting and are amenable to summary for reporting purposes. If we feel that currently the assessment system is likely to lead the task system, it is crucial that the record of assessment is itself driven by the pedagogy that underpins classroom practice.

A useful framework to adopt when assessing performance and understanding owes its origins to the framework for pupil learning outlined in Chapter 5 and allows teachers to differentiate between whether the child has simply experienced an area of the curriculum, is beginning to make sense of the topic or skill or has mastered it.

Schools will have different policies on the degree of detail in record keeping required by different subjects. Nevertheless, detailed record keeping can be justified both as an aid to planning and hence pedagogy and, perhaps increasingly importantly, as a way of ensuring that teacher assessments are given the respect they deserve in summative reporting of pupil achievements.

Detailed record keeping of the kind outlined is rarely found in secondary schools but National Curriculum requirements will both ease the demand on teachers by providing the criteria on which the child is assessed and increase it by expecting teachers to monitor pupil learning in a way that cannot be satisfied by a simple record of work covered. Primary teachers are familiar with checklists of ticks and crosses or different colours to denote the stages towards acquisition or understanding. It now seems that this practice will have to become more common in secondary schools, as assessments have to be recorded more carefully.

Assessing pupils

As we have already indicated, Harlen (1989) notes that mastery of skills is not a simple issue, but may be affected by a child's familiarity with the material to which the skill is to be applied. In addition, most teachers are only too aware of the loss of learning that can occur, even over a half-term break. Consequently, it is important to err on the side of caution when assuming mastery and to ensure that skills and understanding can be demonstrated in a variety of contexts wherever possible. The contexts within which assessments are made are clearly important. Donaldson (1978) alerted the teachers to children's abilities to pick up perceptual cues which may distort their readings of task demands, while motivational factors relating to confidence may also be at work. Edwards (1984, 1988) observed that children as young as 4 years of age had clear ideas about their own competencies in specific areas of the nursery school. Honess, *et al.* (1983) used a personal construct psychology framework to explore the motivational aspects of boys' self-identity and reading performance in poor infant school readers and an adolescent remedial reading group. Evidence suggests that motivational dispositions not only affect performance but are themselves socially constructed both within and outside school. While assessment has to focus on competencies it may be necessary to endeavour to ensure that the learner's feelings about a particular test do not entirely cloud our assessment of his or her ability to use the skills related to that task.

One way of addressing both the mastery and context issues is to gather information on pupil performance from as wide a range of sources as possible. Teachers have been doing this for years through the examination of pupils' written work, observation of performance on task, listening to learners' questions and eavesdropping on conversations while pupils are on task. With national guidelines on learning objectives, the focus of the observations is clearly and uniformly prescribed, consequently the teacher's gaze or ear is geared to note specific aspects of performance. But is it as simple as that? There are several important issues to consider when assessing learners performances on task.

A first concern must be whether we are actually witnessing the optimal performance. Has the pupil in Doyle's terms bid the task down to a low-risk activity? (see Chapters 4 and 5). Many working parents can make a good lasagne, but will microwave a supermarket version at the end of a heavy day. On which 'performance' as chef should he or she be judged? A second issue is whether the child has actually picked out the salient aspect of the task. For example, how easily can a task, which is intended by a teacher to extend and develop vocabulary, become an opportunity to exercise already known routines as the pupils misread and simplify teacher intentions? While these two problems can be overcome through careful goal setting and resourcing, the fundamental issue is the relationship between task setting and assessment.

This relationship is particularly important when teachers decide to place emphasis on process towards outcomes rather than simply final products. Increasingly, teachers are having to focus on 'process goals' in their work with pupils. The National Curriculum makes explicit these demands, as statements of attainment in Mathematics, Science and Design and Technology ask for evidence of the ability to select and use appropriate resources and methods.

The Assessment of Performance Unit (APU) has made interesting attempts to tackle the assessment of process-related skills in the area of Design and Technology (Kelly *et al.*, 1987). Concerned that what they describe as the essence of design and technology might be lost if content and process, or thought and action, are separated, they focused their attentions on the pupil actively engaged in technological tasks. They then isolated a series of stages in such tasks that emphasised process in both understanding and skills. The stages relating to understanding or thought were speculation, exploration, refining and evaluating; those relating to skills or action involved informal drafting, more formalised drafting and experimental modelling, prototyping, and testing and modifying. Clearly these are strongly connected to the learning strategies outlined by Nisbet and Shucksmith (1986) and discussed in Chapter 5 of this book. The lesson from the work of the APU team is that these stages need to be emphasised to the pupils as important process goals that are to be assessed. The power of assessment is obviously an issue, in this case it can be used to place a necessary emphasis on the planning skills demanded by curricula. Once more we return to the relationship between teacher and pupil addressed in Chapter 4 as successful performance and the opportunity to assess these stages depends to a great extent on successful negotiation of desired learning outcomes or goals. Criterion-referenced curricula and related assessments assist the teacher in clarifying appropriate learning outcomes but also make corresponding demands on teacher time for the assessment of pupils. They also require a record-keeping system which supports pedagogy and provides a rigorous link between the assessment of pupil performance and the reporting of that performance.

Rigour at the assessing stage may simply require a sharpening of the looking and listening expertise of teachers, which have already been outlined. Teachers, by tradition and training, are usually good observers of pupils. Sadly the National Curriculum requirements demand a narrowing of focus to concentrate the gaze of specific competencies. A consequent danger may be a fragmented view of the learner in which attention to socio-emotional and physical aspects of the child's development become separated from attention to academic achievement. Record-keeping systems necessarily help in the selection of the assessment focus; consequently a recognition of the need to create a well-balanced profile of each pupil may counteract the possible narrowing of interest.

The assessment skills already available to teachers are shown in Table 8.1.

Table 8.1 **Using teacher skills in assessing pupils' work**

Teacher skills	Applications	Techniques	Weaknesses
Observation skills	Activities involving selection of resources, construction, sorting, some planning activities	Diary notes checklists photographs	Teacher can miss points when 'distracted'. 'Doing' doesn't necessarily mean full understanding
Listening skills	Activities involving oracy skills demonstrating understanding of concepts, e.g. through giving explanations or planning	Diary notes, checklists, Tape recordings, Diagnostic 'conversations'	Difficult to get close to learners without interrupting. Teacher questions can lead responses. Pupils can be wary of teacher questions and under-perform
Marking written skills	Activities involving writing and including cloze procedures, plans and simple paper and pencil tests	Diary notes, checklists, examples of pupils' work	Pupils' written explanations do not do justice to their conceptual understanding. Can force an emphasis on the final product to the detriment of the quality of the process skills

The techniques we have suggested demonstrate the wide variety of ways in which teachers can use existing skills and collect evidence of pupils' competencies in a relatively rigorous manner. Photographs of prototypes and completed constructions and examples of written planning or final products not only serve as more lasting reminders of learners' competencies but may be selectively retained to supplement profiles of pupil progress through the curriculum.

Tape recordings may be used for similar purposes but are more likely to be of use when providing evidence of pupils' abilities without the presence of the teacher. Open-ended but carefully resourced problem-solving tasks may seem suited to this method of information collection. However, the danger here is that there may be the need for a lot of teacher listening time in order to catch a few pieces of hard evidence. Indeed, it appears that this method works best when a simple task, for example measuring or mixing, is set, or when children are asked to engage in a specific planning activity perhaps relating to oracy skills and story telling. Another good use of the tape recorder is to supply a pupil or pair of pupils with a task and an instruction card which requires them to record responses at certain key points during the task.

What is evident from Table 8.1 is that no assessment skill or technique is without its problems. Therefore, we return to the point made earlier, that it is necessary to collect information in a variety of ways and in different contexts.

Profiles and records of achievement

As we move on to consider the reporting of assessments it is interesting to observe the development of pupil profiling in secondary schooling during the 1980s. Profiles emerged as a heartfelt response to what is frequently described as the pernicious effects of the secondary school examination system which was regarded as depersonalising and demotivating. A range of models for profiles were created (see Law (1984) for an overview). While all shared a common emphasis on building a rounded and developmental picture of the pupil, they differed in the amount of responsibility for assessment given to pupils, parents and teachers. In some cases they were jointly controlled by pupil and teacher and assessments negotiated between both. Other models represented an extension of the more traditional teacher reporting and others supplemented this method with supplied teacher comments from comment banks in attempts to avoid what was regarded by some as the subjectivity of negotiated assessment of the idiosyncracies of teachers' own written comments.

The control of profiles is an interesting area which can only be briefly addressed here (see Hargreaves (1986) for a critical perspective on the profiling movement). Nevertheless, it is important to consider the pedagogical implications of jointly negotiated assessments, particularly when this is considered in the light of the emphasis we have given to classroom interactions and negotiations around task setting in earlier chapters of this book. Indeed, jointly controlled assessments under a profiling scheme may have considerable effect on the teaching–learning interaction in classrooms as goals and interpretations are more fully explained. Once again we have an example of how the assessment system may be used to lead the task system, as this particular form of assessment may induct pupils into metacognitive reflection on their own learning processes. Systems of supported self-study, for example, regard review, assessment and evaluation of pupils' work in the tutorial element of the programme as extremely powerful opportunities for learning.

The use of profiles and records of achievement fits well with the framework for assessment underpinning this chapter. We have differentiated between formative and summative assessment, and have more finely explored the difference between diagnostic and more general formative statements of pupil achievements. We have been suggesting that detailed record keeping based on formative assessment is necessary for effective lesson planning and task setting but that these are essentially private documents of use primarily to the teacher. They do, however, provide the information that may be distilled into more general developmental profiles to allow an accumulative record of the child's progress through schooling as he or she moves from term to term and from class to class. This itself feeds the final summative record that is given to the pupil on leaving school in order to provide information for employers or the next stage of education.

Profiles therefore carry summative information for public consumption by parents and colleagues. The information they hold may also be summarised into a final report or reference format at the end of schooling. While currently formats vary there is generally an emphasis on producing a well-balanced view of the pupil which allows consideration not only of academic progress but also of social and physical development. As the portrait is cumulative, extending throughout the child's school life, another concern is simplicity and readability and the appropriateness of the design for both school entry and transfer requirements. These summaries may be supplemented by hard evidence, for example items of pupil work. In this way information used for more detailed formative assessment is used to illuminate and give depth to the profile portraits.[3]

Clearly profiles serve an important purpose but need to be seen as simply a method of reporting pupil progress. Assessment occurs during the daily processes of classroom life and needs to be recorded in ways that support the daily professional decision making of teachers.

In the UK the profiling movement has suffered a series of setbacks. Broadfoot (1984), in an interesting comparison between England and Wales and France, notes that the heavily centrally controlled French system of education has made considerable strides away from more formal examinations towards pupil profiling while the less centralised system in England and Wales in the early 1980s resulted in a more ferocious clinging to control through examinations. Now that it has been decided that Records of Achievement are not to be the compulsory form of reporting achievement in British schools it would appear that, in the UK, increasing centralisation of education is not producing a parallel tendency to profiling as a counter-balance.

Self-evaluation in classrooms

Earlier in this chapter we touched upon the problems of accountability inherent in too simplistic a view of the relationship between pupil performance and the evaluation of curricula institutions or the practice of teaching. The relationship between assessment and evaluation is in fact a subtle one and may be seen as empowering for both pupil and teacher.

Evaluation is essentially a simple process, best illustrated as a cycle of review, plan, act and review, as shown in Figure 8.1.

Figure 8.1 **The plan–act–review cycle**

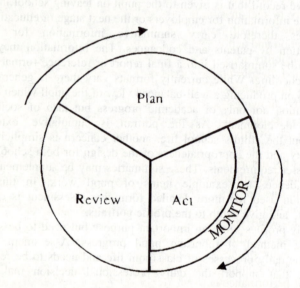

Planning involves setting clear, achievable goals based on review. This is followed by taking action which is aimed at ensuring the realisation of these goals, monitoring that action and finally reviewing the outcome of the action in terms of the original goals. The review stage demands reflection on whether or not the goals set have been met and the reasons for whatever disparity exists. This reflection forms the starting point for planning the next action stage.

This model of evaluation is frequently used by teachers in the daily monitoring and planning of classroom tasks. Interestingly it also can provide a useful framework for pupils' management of their own learning. As we outlined in Chapter 1, major themes in this volume include pupil motivation, metacognition, or reflection on one's own learning, and self-evaluation. We can begin to see how they are closely related. To return to a point we have already made several times, clearly defined goals have to be linked to an interactive model of pedagogy if children are to perform to the best of their ability in any curricular area. When this is considered, using the language of evaluation, we are suggesting that goals are clearly set or negotiated and that pupil progress towards goals may be monitored by both teachers and the pupils themselves. Also the degree of success as the goal is reached is open to evaluation by pupils. Self-evaluating pupils, therefore, are able to take greater responsibility for their own learning processes (see Nisbet and Shucksmith, 1986; Waterhouse, 1988). Similarly, as we have already argued, self-evaluating teachers are more likely to feel in control of their own decision making. Taylor (1977) points to a strong and important link between responsibility, self-evaluation and action and motivation, regarding the opportunity to take responsibility for evaluations of one's own actions as crucial to motivation. Edwards (1988) related this to schools in terms of the quality of the relationship between learner and teacher. Motivating children by allowing them increasing responsibility for their own evaluations requires a delicate handling of interactions and the avoidance of overtly judgemental behaviours on the part of the teacher.

It may be unfair to ask practitioners to assess without being judgemental. Nevertheless, the demotivating effect of depressed pupil self-esteem due to experience of failure needs to be considered. Careful match of task and child based on assessment of learning needs should help avoid situations in which self-esteem is threatened by failure on task, while clear goal setting encourages pupil self-evaluation. Some of the difficulties of an over-emphasis on assessment nevertheless do continue as teachers are under pressure to produce good pupil performances in specific areas of the curriculum to satisfy the external evaluations of their pedagogy and of their institutions.

For both pupils and teachers the route to a feeling of effectiveness is a feeling of control over processes and outcomes or, put more simply, the ability to predict future results. We all know the apprehension with which we approach, for example, a new and complex appliance or tackle a new recipe that demands untested skills. We fear the possibility of our own ineffectiveness, and may delay tackling the new appliance or decide to try out the recipe for our nearest and dearest before risking the demonstration of our ineptitude to the wider world. We have already noted in Chapter 5 that a pupil response to this kind of challenge in classrooms is to attempt to remove the risk by bidding down the task, so that instead of being a challenge it becomes routine. If, as teachers, we want to keep some element of challenge in some tasks, we need to provide pupils with coping strategies which allow them to keep the activity within their control. One way is to allow them to take responsibility for some evaluations. As we have already suggested, the learning strategies outlined by Nisbet and Shucksmith (1986), and summarised in the notion of 'planfulness', fit well with the plan–act–review cycle and allow the child to break activities into manageable stages of, for example, planning, monitoring, checking, revising and self-testing (Nisbet and Shucksmith, 1986, p. 28).

Similarly, teachers may feel overwhelmed or pressured by the challenging demands of a nationally imposed and planned curriculum. One way of keeping a grip on process in a time of change has always been to self-monitor, to use consistently the plan–act–review cycle when initiating change in the classroom. With the increase in accountability through the implementation of a national curriculum, and to an extent through teacher appraisal, there is also a need to be increasingly articulate in the justification of pedagogic practices. Regular use of the evaluation cycle with its emphasis on monitoring and reflection on action, allows practitioners to stand back and examine their own practices, to discover ways of explaining them and to keep a record of curricular and pedagogic decisions they have made. All three aspects empower teachers when they enter the arena of external or public evaluation of their teaching or institution.[4]

Teacher professionalism and accountability

The tension between public accountability and professional integrity can be seen in the areas of both assessment and evaluation. Both issues demand demonstration and public recognition of teachers' professional competence. Without public recognition of their professional competence in the areas of assessment and evaluation, teachers will be unable to resist further intervention by the government, or by the governors of their own school. Hard evidence will be needed. In the case of pupil assessment this will be found in the quality of the assessment process demonstrated in effective record keeping. In the case of evaluation, written records are also important. They need to be simple and relevant, and take up as little time as possible. Models of teacher appraisal that are primarily concerned with staff development have already picked up on these points. Those appraisal systems which require the teacher to engage in self-evaluation prior to and during appraisal are premised on the belief that teachers need to enter into appraisal or external evaluation as active participants who see themselves – and are seen – as able to use the experience to extend their own understanding, and hence to increase the effectiveness of their teaching. Written evidence, such as a summary of a diary record of the monitoring of action, taken together with reflections and planning, provide an agenda for discussion. Consequently, the professional is able to take some control over that agenda and discuss what he or she sees to be most relevant. Here we return to the notion of responsibility we have just discussed in connection with pupil learning. Logically this leads us to stress the importance of teachers also being responsible for their own evaluations of their actions if teachers are to take and pursue pedagogic decisions.

Notes and further reading

1. A sound basic explanatory text which picks up on National Curriculum issues, GCSE, and profiling is Desforges (1989).
2. Several papers in a British Educational Research Association publication elaborate the debates surrounding national assessment, (see, for example, Torrance (1988). Two references that discuss wider issues not covered in this chapter, including work-based learning, graded testing and other technical topics in the area of assessment, are Black and Dockrell (1988) and Brown (1989). Broadfoot (1984) explores historical, cross-cultural and the more general sociological issues relating to assessment.
3. A useful practical guide to developing records of achievement is found in Pritchard and Richmond (1989), and Broadfoot (1986) has edited a wide-ranging overview of developments in records of achievement at both a practical and critical level.
4. A good introduction to issues relating to school, curriculum and teacher evaluation is provided by Horton and Raggat (1982). Similarly important basic issues, relating institutional and self-evaluation to accountability, are raised in Nuttall (1981) and Simons (1987).

Seminar suggestions

1. Ask students to think of an activity they have recently planned, given, or might consider giving to a group of learners in a classroom. It can be mundane or imaginative, for example writing a letter, gathering information, making a model. Ask them to list the competencies (skills/understanding) that the pupils may demonstrate on that task. Then ask students to focus on one or two competencies and decide on how they would assess mastery of the competency, for example through observation, examination of written work.

   Discussion could focus on the need to isolate aspects of the learner's performance when assessing, sharing these goals with the pupil, appropriate methods of assessing, building assessment into task planning, or avoiding waste of teacher time.

2. Ask students to provide examples of pupils' work. (Equally these can be supplied by the tutor.) In each case the intended outcomes or pedagogical purposes of the task should be made clear in an explanatory paragraph. Ask students to work in pairs or threes to assess the learner's performance on the task, answering the question 'What is it evident that the pupil can do?' Then ask each pair or triad to note the difficulties they have had with the task. In a final plenary discussion the following issues could be raised: the importance of relationships to our assessment of learners, for example how well we know the pupil; the expectations we hold; the asssessment skills teachers possess and use without self-awareness; the need to be clear about intended task outcomes; agreement on mastery of a competency; the 'whole person' view of education; the irrelevance of the age of the pupil to criterion-referenced testing; the implications for record keeping.

3. Ask students to think of an activity they have planned recently for a group of pupils. Ask them to identify the aim of the activity, and of how they knew that the aim had been met (or not), what they as teachers had learned from setting that task and how they might do it differently next time. Discuss the importance of monitoring and collecting evidence about the action taken to provide a focus for reflection and planning and remind students of ways in which evidence may be collected, for example, observations, diary, tape recording, photographs, pupils' work, talking with pupils or parents. Provide groups of three students with large sheets of paper and pens and ask them to work through the review–plan–act–review cycle on one of the activities described, this time emphasising how and where evidence may be collected – for example: What needs to be considered at the planning stage? Where can evidence be gathered? What is an appropriate way of monitoring the activity, and one that does not take up too much teacher time? Who can help with the review or reflection stage? What do you really need to know at that stage? Were the aims clearly stated at the planning stage?

    The session could finish with a discussion on either the importance of having clear aims in order to evaluate effectively, or on appropriate methods of monitoring actions.

Chapter 9

Conclusions

Theory and classroom practice: an interactive relationship

Chapter 1 argued that theories provide starting points from which we can begin to reflect on, monitor and evaluate our own experience. This is particularly true when their theoretical underpinning enables researchers to obtain results the significance of which extends beyond the research sample itself. Examples are Bennett's work on matching the difficulty of the task to the ability of the pupil (Bennett *et al.*, 1986, Ch. 5), the extensive investigations into time on task (*op. cit.*, Ch. 6) and the even more extensive investigations into applied behaviour analysis (*op. cit.*, Ch. 6).

Yet the relationship is not one way. The problems teachers face in the classroom can also provoke theoretical advances. The Warnock Report's conclusion that up to 20 per cent of children could be said to have special educational needs (DES, 1978a) and the claim of HMI in Scotland that up to 50 per cent of pupils could be said to have learning difficulties (SED, 1978) directed both professional and political attention to the needs of academically less able pupils. Nevertheless, it was the experience of teachers in mainstream schools that provided the impetus for a radical reformulation of the scope and aims of education for the children concerned, with consequent developments in the conceptual framework for its provision.

In other words, theory and research interact with classroom practice. This view can be looked at from two angles. First, although politicians play a part – perhaps an unhealthily large part – in determining the allocation of research funds, in practice research teams have to modify their agenda in the light of teachers' current interests. The reason is simply that teachers quite reasonably withhold active cooperation from researchers who are not addressing their legitimate concerns. Secondly, and more importantly, the models of teaching and learning that we have proposed in this book place the teacher in the role of researcher. The monitoring, reappraisal and self-evaluation inherent in all effective teaching is essentially a research activity.[1]

Teachers as learners

The interactive relationship between teachers and researchers implies, then, that teachers influence the agenda for research, often after it has formally been defined by politicians or by researchers themselves. It also implies that teachers determine the nature of theoretical advances in the obvious, but important, sense that most major advances in school and teacher effectiveness have been based on researchers' observations of teachers at work. We have given particular emphasis to four themes throughout this book.

1. The influences on children's development are varied, and interact on each other. Returning to children with special needs, Rutter (1981) points out that children can cope with single, isolated sources of stress, however severe, if they really are isolated. In contrast, when sources of stress come in combination – for example, when parental separation is combined with financial problems in the home, a change of house, death of a loved grandparent *and* a string of supply teachers in a school that suffers from weak leadership – the effects of each is likely to interact with and aggravate the other. Most teachers can think of children whose behaviour and progress have deteriorated when several things in their lives have gone wrong at the same time. Similarly, most can recognise the potential impact of culturally based expectations connected with gender, ethnicity and social class. Gender and ethnicity are currently politically more sensitive – or at least talked about more. On the other hand, it remains quite clear that children from working-class homes are likely to leave school with fewer qualifications than those from middle-class homes, irrespective of intellectual ability (e.g. Davie *et al.*, 1972; Fogelman, 1976).

2. Teaching is a process in which children and teachers interact with, and on, each other. Again, most teachers will recognise the reciprocity described, for example, by Doyle (1986). The interaction can be constructive – a necessary and desirable aspect of working together on a shared task – or it can be restricting, as when children successfully negotiate down the difficulty of a task.

3. A hallmark of successful teaching is that children develop the metacognitive skills of reflecting critically on the nature of a task, monitoring the demands it makes and identifying appropriate ways to overcome them. However, children are only likely to acquire these skills when their teacher has acquired them, and uses them in his or her own teaching.

4. It follows from this that evaluation is central to all teaching activities. The evaluation can be carried out at several levels. Failure to differentiate adequately between the needs of different children or groups of children can lead to unstimulating, undemanding tasks for able children and tasks which less able children find too difficult. In other words, attention focuses both on the abilities of the children and on the difficulty of the task. At

a slightly more complex level, failure to recognise our own personal biases, perhaps arising from cultural expectations linked to gender, race or social class, can lead us to expect too little of some children and, possibly, too much of others.

All this raises important questions about the applications of research. Clearly, there is no direct relationship between research findings and changes in professional practice. If all schools could become more effective simply by copying the most effective schools described by Rutter *et al.* (1979), teaching would be a boringly mechanistic and straightforward process. It manifestly is not! Hence, we need to consider the processes that restrict and enhance our ability and/or willingness to learn from our own or other people's experience. The concept of motivational style is helpful here.

Motivation to learn: an attributionist perspective

Motivational style develops from teachers' and children's perceptions of the environment in which they work. According to Ames (1987) it is the systematic, qualitative response that individuals make to situations in which they judge success or failure to be possible. These perceptions are held to determine the 'style' of the individual's motivation. The concept of style is useful because it moves away from quantitative definitions of motivation such as time on task. Instead it sees children as actively involved in making choices about how they will behave. Two forms of motivational style have particular relevance for teachers.

'Learned helplessness'

Some children believe they are not clever enough to succeed on a task and rapidly give up. Because they attribute failure to lack of ability, their expectation of success rapidly declines: they do not believe there is any point in trying (see Dweck and Wortman, 1982). Dweck also identifies another group of children whom she defines as 'mastery oriented'. These children do not attribute failure to lack of ability; rather, when they have found something difficult they seek clues as to how they may improve their performance in future.

Self-worth motivation

Other children believe they *are* clever enough to succeed on a task but do not want to risk failure. Because being clever, successful or popular is important to their self-esteem they avoid situations in which their image of themselves could be threatened. For these children, the harder they try at a task, for example coursework for GCSE, the greater the threat to their self-esteem if they do not succeed. Secondary teachers may see this in its most extreme form in lower attaining pupils in years 10 to 11 (14 to 16 year-olds). These pupils sometimes form themselves into a group which consciously rejects the school's aims and values.[2] In effect, these pupils are protecting themselves from failure by refusing to make any real effort. Younger pupils also adopt this strategy, claiming that they are not interested or 'don't care'. Older pupils make the same claim, but an additional and perhaps more powerful influence is the need for approval from other, similarly disaffected, young people.

A controversy in research on motivational style concerns how it becomes established. Children do not behave in the same way with all teachers. A child who appears successful and highly motivated in one subject may show all the signs of learned helplessness or self-worth protection in another. Nicholls (1984) has suggested that motivational style crystallises around the age of 11. This could be due to developmental factors and/or to changes in school organisation. Young children's conceptions of ability allow for the possibility that it may increase. After puberty they may increasingly see ability as relatively fixed and stable. This is, however, a gradual process, which probably results from an interaction between developmental and environmental factors.

For secondary school teachers there are two implications. First, as they get older pupils may become increasingly sensitive to models of school organisation which, intentionally or otherwise, identify them as 'successes' or 'failures'. This is likely to happen when pupils in lower ability groups believe that their teachers would prefer to be teaching the 'A' band or a higher set. With the start of GCSE course work, if not before, movement between groups becomes difficult; thus pupils have good reason for doubting whether effort will be rewarded. As they become increasingly able to recognise the long-term effects of ability grouping, it is not altogether surprising that they come to regard ability as relatively fixed and stable. Secondly, teaching methods that rely on formal instruction do little to encourage pupils to see themselves as having responsibility for their own learning. It follows that they may increasingly come to attribute their progress, or lack of progress, to factors over which they have no control. If they attribute it to their own lack of ability we could predict increasingly frequent indications of learned helplessness. If they attribute it to the school's organisation and curriculum, we could predict increasingly frequent indications of self-worth motivation.

As so often happens, children's strategies, or in this case motivational styles, have a parallel in those of their teachers. Learned helplessness is reflected in comments like 'he's just not very bright, and that's all there is to it', or 'her problem is her parents and we can't change *them*'. Such comments conceal a feeling that nothing the individual does will make any difference, either in the sense of eliciting support from senior colleagues or in terms of pupil progress. Ultimately this leads to loss of interest in the professional nature of the job and the feeling of apathy associated with 'burn-out'.[3]

Self-worth motivation, or more descriptively self-worth protection, is reflected in comments like: 'I *could* do something for Jenny but it wouldn't be fair on the others to give her so much time', or 'I *could* do something for Peter but it would be undermined by parental indifference, so there's no point'. Self-worth motivation is seen in teachers who hide behind their professional status to justify reluctance to evaluate their work. It may also be seen in teachers who use their, perhaps legitimate, sense of grievance about inadequate resources or poor conditions of service to justify low levels of involvement in their work.

Changing and/or maintaining motivational style

So far we have only drawn attention to the potentially restricting, negative effects of motivational style. Most teachers, though, approach their work in ways that create opportunities not only for their pupils but also for their own professional development, rather than restricting them in the way envisaged by learned helplessness and self-worth motivation. Hence, we need to ask how a positive motivational style can be maintained as well as how a less positive one may be changed.

Diener and Dweck (1978) demonstrated the possibility of reducing the effects of learned helplessness. Although they were working with primary age boys, their work also has obvious relevance for secondary teachers. They gave children who had been identified as learned helpless a test on which failure was likely. They then told one group that they had not tried hard enough, and should make greater effort in a second test. The second group was told that the first test had been difficult, but was congratulated for trying. The theory of learned helplessness predicts that the second group's performance will deteriorate still further on the second test, because the teacher has reinforced their own belief in their lack of ability to influence what happens to them: if the task is likely to be difficult, there is no point in trying. In contrast the theory would predict that the first group might improve on the second test: the children had been told that their failure was something they *could* do something about, by trying harder. This, in fact, is what happened. The implication is that children who feel that *they* have some control over their own learning are likely to develop a sense of responsibility for it. In Doyle's terms, children are more likely to take risks if they see their teacher as someone who helps them to achieve mastery in spite of the difficulties (Doyle and

Carter, 1984; Doyle, 1986). In Nisbet and Shucksmith's (1986) terms, metacognitive skills give children a feeling of involvement in and responsibility for their work, which is incompatible with the restrictions on development implicit in learned helplessness and self-worth motivation.

There is a lack of systematic research on the motivational styles of teachers, let alone on ways of changing them. On the other hand, both anecdote and observation suggests that motivational style is not constant. Rather it responds to the quality of leadership and support from colleagues, and to the nebulous concept of school climate.

There is now a growing body of research on differences between schools in pupils' behaviour and educational progress, irrespective of the social background of the school's pupils. It is equally clear that schools are not static institutions. For better or worse, many schools vary over time in their effectiveness in achieving their educational and social goals. It is reasonable to suppose that developments in pupil performance reflect developments in teachers' motivation. One implication that merits further investigation is that motivational style may be related to the concepts of morale and job satisfaction.

School effectiveness research has repeatedly drawn attention to the crucial importance of the head teacher (e.g. Rutter *et al.*, 1979). There is very limited evidence on the relationship between a school's effectiveness and the management style of the head. Galloway (1983) described pastoral care in four secondary schools with exceptionally low rates of disruptive behaviour. In two he described the head teacher's management style as autocratic, in another democratic and in the remaining school as mixed. The common theme, though, was that:

the head-teacher communicated his philosophy and goals to teachers and through them to pupils and to the community. Teachers mostly felt that their problems were understood, and their efforts and achievements respected. Decisions might be autocratic but they were not arbitrary. (p. 252)

It would be surprising, then, if differences between schools, both in teachers' job satisfaction and in their effectiveness in helping pupils to meet their educational and social goals, were unrelated to the quality of guidance and leadership provided by senior staff.

The guidance and leadership that senior staff provide should itself be based on a clear educational philosophy with a coherent psychological rationale. A study in New Zealand found that school principals who were currently undertaking some form of advanced professional study, either through a university course or correspondence course, reported significantly higher job satisfaction than those who were not (Galloway *et al.*, 1986). The numbers were small, so conclusions must be tentative. We are not suggesting that if only all teachers would enrol for post-experience degree or diploma courses at their local college or university, the nation's educational problems would be solved. Two possible implications are nevertheless interesting: (a) advanced professional study may promote the model of the self-evaluating, questioning teacher that is implicit in so much of the work we have discussed in earlier chapters: (b) this approach to teaching from senior staff promotes a positive motivational style, not only in the senior teachers themselves, but also in their colleagues and in pupils.

Overview

The usefulness of the work of academics studying the psychology of education may be judged largely by the extent to which it helps teachers to raise the quality of their work with children. The same is true of the work of educational psychologists employed by LEAs. Children's learning processes, and the factors that influence them, are as likely to retain a central place in the work of psychologists, as of teachers. In other words, teachers and psychologists have a shared interest in the influence on children's educational, personal and social development of schools as social organisations and of the classroom as an environment for learning. The partnership between teaching and psychology has been a profitable one in the past. In the 1990s it will assume even greater importance. The 1980s saw central control of education increase beyond recognition, culminating in the 1988 Education Reform Act. The National Curriculum, local management of schools, the possibility of seeking grant-maintained status, increased parental freedom to select their child's school, etc., are legislative changes that were ostensibly motivated by a desire to raise educational standards. Yet legislation can do nothing more than provide the framework within which the education system develops. Development is not necessarily healthy, and as we have already noted it is too early to evaluate the impact of the 1988 Act.

Nevertheless, we feel no embarrassment in concluding with two suggestions. First, every LEA has plenty of examples of what HMI is pleased to call 'good practice', both at school and at classroom level. While the concept of good practice is contentious, not least because it varies over time,[4] the evidence that schools vary in their success in achieving common educational and social goals is now widely accepted. The evidence also suggests that variations between teachers within a school are at least as important as variation between schools. An increasingly clear picture is emerging of effective schools and of effective teachers. Secondly, the successful introduction of the National Curriculum, together with all the other changes the government imposed in the 1980s, will demand an increasingly sophisticated understanding of teaching and learning processes. Substantial progress has been made. A disquieting characteristic of this progress is that the more we understand about teaching and learning the more clearly we recognise how much remains to be understood. This *is* disquieting, but it is also why most teachers will enjoy their work: opportunities for personal and professional development continue throughout the individual's career. We hope this book will help to open up some of these opportunities.

Notes and further reading

1. The notion of teachers as researchers is well developed in Stenhouse (1975).
2. For a more detailed description of this process from a sociological perspective see Willis (1977) and Hargreaves (1967).
3. The concept of burn-out is more fully explored in Edelwick and Brodsky (1980).
4. The controversies on what constitutes good practice are well analysed by Knight and Smith (1989).

Seminar suggestions

1. Debate the motion that: 'Public money spent on employing educational psychologists and on research into the psychology of education would be better spent in other ways'.
2. Think of two children you have taught whose behaviour is consistent with 'learned helplessness' or 'self-worth motivated' as described in the text. Be prepared to describe the children in the seminar, and discuss ways in which you might increase their motivation to attempt challenging tasks in the classroom.

BIBLIOGRAPHY

Ainscow, M. and Florek, A. (eds) (1989) *Special Educational Needs: Towards a Whole-School Approach*. London, David Fulton.

Ames, C. (1987) The enhancement of student motivation. In M. Maehr and D.A. Kleiber (eds) *Enhancing Motivation*. Greenwich, Conn., JAI Press.

Anderson, E. (1973) *The Disabled Schoolchild; A Study of Integration in Primary Schools*. London, Methuen.

Anderson, L.W. (ed.) (1986) *Time and School Learning*. London, Croom Helm.

Apple, M. (1979) *Ideology and the Curriculum*. London, Routledge and Kegan Paul.

Apple, M. (1983) *Power and Education*. London, Routledge and Kegan Paul.

Apple, M. (1985) *Education and Power*. London, Ark.

Association for Science Education (ASE) (1988) *Initiatives in Primary Science: An Evaluation. Building Bridges*. Hatfield, ASE.

ASE (Association for Science Education together with Association of Teachers of Mathematics, Mathematical Association, and National Association for the teaching of English) (1989) *The National Curriculum – Making it Work for the Primary School*. Hatfield, ASE.

Ausubel, D. (1968) *Educational Psychology: A Cognitive View*. New York, Holt, Rinehart and Winston.

Baldwin, J. and Wells, H. (1979) *Active Tutorial Work: Book 1, The First Year – Book 5, The Fifth Year*. Oxford, Blackwell.

Bandura, A. (1974) Behaviour theory and models of man. *American Psychologist*, 29, 859–69.

Bannister, D. and Fransella, F. (1971) *Inquiring Man: The Theory of Personal Constructs*. Harmondsworth, Penguin.

Barnes, D. (1976) *From Communication to Curriculum*. Harmondsworth, Penguin.

Barnes, D. and Todd, F. (1977) *Curriculum and Learning in Small Groups*. London, Routledge and Kegan Paul.

Barton, L. (1988) (ed.) *The Politics of Special Educational Needs*. Lewes, Falmer Press.

Barton, L. (1989) *Special Educational Needs: Myth or Reality?* Lewes, Falmer Press.

Barton, L. and Meighan, R. (1978) *Sociological Interpretations of Schooling and Classrooms: a reappraisal*. Driffield, Nafferton.

Barton L. and Tomlinson, S. (eds) (1984) *Special Education and Social Interests*. London, Croom Helm.

Bates, R.V. (1984) Educational versus managerial evaluation in schools. In M.P. Broadfoot (ed.) *Selection, Certification and Control: Social Issues in Educational Assessment*. Lewes, Falmer Press.

Bennett, N. (1985a) Interaction and achievement in classroom groups. In N. Bennett and C. Desforges (eds) *Recent Advances in Classroom Research*. Edinburgh, Scottish Academic Press.

Bennett, N. (1985b) Time to teach: teaching-learning processes in primary schools. In N.J. Entwistle (ed.) *New Directions in Educational Psychology – Learning and Teaching*. Lewes, Falmer Press.

Bennett, N. and Blundell, D. (1983) Quantity and quality of work in rows and classroom groups. *Educational Psychology*, 3, 93–105.

Bennett, N., Desforges, C., Cockburn, A. and Wilkinson, B. (1984) *The Quality of Pupil Learning Experiences*. London, Lawrence Erlbaum.

Berger, M. (1979) Behaviour modification in education and professional practice: the dangers of a mindless technology. *Bulletin of the British Psychological Society*, 32, 418–19.

Berger, M. (1982) Applied behaviour analysis in education: a critical assessment and some implications for teachers. *Educational Psychology*, 2, 289–300.

Berliner, D.C. (1987) Ways of thinking about students and classrooms by more and less experienced teachers. In J. Calderhead (ed.) *Exploring Teachers' Thinking*. London, Cassell.

Best, R., Jarvis, C. and Ribbins, P. (1980) (eds) *Perspectives on Pastoral Care*. London, Heinemann.

Best, R., Ribbins, P., Jarvis, C. with Oddy, D. (1983) *Education and Care*. London, Heinemann.

Beveridge, M. (ed.) (1982) *Children Thinking Through Language*. London, Edward Arnold.

Black, H.D. and Dockrell, W.B. (eds) (1988) *New Developments in Educational Assessment*. Edinburgh, Scottish Academic Press.

Bourdieu, P. (1977) Cultural Reproduction and Social Reproduction. In J. Karabel and A. H. Halsey (eds) *Power and Ideology in Education*. New York, Oxford University Press.

Bower, G.H. and Hildegard, E.R. (1981) *Theories of Learning*. Englewood Cliffs, NJ, Prentice-Hall.

Bowles, S. and Gintis, H. (1976) *Schooling in Capitalist America*. London, Routledge and Kegan Paul.

Boydell, D. (1975) Pupil behaviour in junior classrooms. *British Journal of Educational Psychology*, 45, 122–9.

Broadfoot, P. (ed.) (1984) *Selection, Certification and Control: Social Issues in Educational Assessment*. Lewes, Falmer Press.

Broadfoot, P. (ed.) (1986) *Profiles and Records of Achievement: A Review of Issues and Practice*. Eastbourne, Holt, Rinehart and Winston.

Broadfoot, P. (1988) The national assessment framework and records of achievement. In H. Torrance (ed.) *National Assessment and Testing: A Research Response*. Kendal, British Educational Research Association.

Brown, M. (1989) Graded assessment and learning hierarchies in mathematics – an alternative view. *British Educational Research Journal*, 15, (2), 121–8.

Brown, A. and De Loache, J. (1983) Metacognitive skills. In M. Donaldson, R. Grieve and C. Pratt (eds) *Early Childhood Development and Education*. Oxford, Blackwell.

Brown, G. and Desforges, C. (1979) *Piaget's Theory: A Psychological Critique*. London, Routledge and Kegan Paul.

Brown, G.A. and Edmondson, R. (1984) Asking questions. In E.C. Wragg (ed.) *Classroom Teaching Skills*. London, Croom Helm.

Bruner, J.S. (1966) *Towards a Theory of Instruction*. Cambridge, Mass, CUP.

Bruner, J.S. (1974) *Beyond the Information Given*. London, Allen and Unwin.

Bruner, J.S. (1986) *Actual Minds, Possible Worlds*. Cambridge, Mass., Harvard University Press.

Button, L. (1981) *Group Tutoring for the Form Teacher: A Developmental Model, Book 1: Lower Secondary School; Book 2: Upper Secondary School*. London, Hodder and Stoughton.

Central Advisory Council on Education (CACE) (1967) *Children and their Primary Schools* (The Plowden Report). London, HMSO.

Callaghan, J. (1976) *Speech by the Prime Minister*, the Rt Hon. James Callaghan MP, at a foundation stone-laying ceremony at Ruskin College, Oxford, on Monday, 18 October (press release).

Carlberg, C. and Kavale, K. (1980) Efficacy of special versus regular class placement for exceptional children: a meta-analysis. *Journal of Special Education*, 14, 295–309.

Carter, K. and Doyle, W. (1987) Teachers' knowledge structures and comprehension processes. In J. Calderhead (ed.) *Exploring Teachers' Thinking*. London, Cassell.

Chapman, P.D. (1981) Schools as sorters: testing and tracking in California, 1910–1925. *Journal of Social History*, 14, 701–17.

Chi, M.T.H. (1978) Knowledge structures and memory development. In R.S. Seiger (ed.) *Children's Thinking: What Develops?* Hillsdale, Lawrence Erlbaum.

Chi, M.T.H. (1981) Knowledge development and memory performance. In M.P. Friedman, J.P. Das and N. O'Connor (eds) *Intelligence and Learning*. New York, Plenum Press.

Claxton, G., Swann, W., Salmon, P., Walkerdine, V., Jacobsen, B. and White, J. (1985) *Psychology and Schooling: What's the Matter?* Bedford Way Papers, 25. London, University of London Institute of Education.

Cohen, L. and Manion, L. (1981) *Perspectives on Schools and Classrooms.* London, Holt, Rinehart and Winston.

Cole, M. (1985) The zone of proximal development: where culture and cognition create each other. In J.V. Wertsch (ed.) *Culture Communication and Cognition.* Cambridge, Cambridge University Press.

Coleman, J.S. and Hendry, L. (1990) *The Nature of Adolescence* (2nd edn). London, Routledge.

Coleman, J.S. *et al.* (1966) *Equality of Educational Opportunity.* Washington, US Government Printing Office.

Craik, F.I.M. and Tulving, E. (1975) Depth of processing and the retention of words in episodic memory. *Journal of Experimental Psychology*, 104, 268–94.

Croll, P. and Moses, D. (1988) Teaching methods and time on task in junior classrooms. *Educational Research*, 30, 90–7.

David, K. and Charlton, T. (eds) (1987) *The Caring Role of the Primary School.* London, Macmillan.

Davie, R., Butler, N. and Goldstein, H. (1972) *From Birth to Seven.* London, Longman.

Deem, R. (1986) Gender and social class. In R. Rogers (ed.) *Education and Social Class.* Lewes, Falmer Press.

Delamont, S. and Galton, M. (1986) *Inside the Secondary Classroom.* London, Routledge and Kegal Paul.

Department of Education and Science (DES) (1975) *The Discovery of Children Requiring Special Education and the Assessment of their Needs.* (Circular 2/75). London, DES.

Department of Education and Science (DES) (1978a) *Special Educational Needs.* (The Warnock Report.) London, HMSO.

Department of Education and Science (DES) (1978b) *Primary Education in England.* London, HMSO.

Department of Education and Science (DES) (1981) *West Indian Children in Our Schools.* (Interim Report of the Committee of Inquiry into the Education of Children from Ethnic Minority Groups. Chairman Anthony Rampton.) London, HMSO.

Department of Education and Science (DES) (1982) *Mathematics Counts.* (Report of the Committee of Inquiry into the Teaching of Mathematics in Schools. Chairman W.H. Cockcroft.) London, HMSO.

Department of Education and Science (DES) (1985) *Better Schools.* London, HMSO.

Department of Education and Science (DES) (1988a) *School Teachers' Pay and Conditions of Service Document.* London, DES.

Department of Education and Science (DES) (1988b) *LEA Training*

Grants Scheme: Training to Meet the Special Educational Needs of Pupils with Learning Difficulties in Schools: Guidance Note (Teacher Training Circular Letter 1/88). London, DES.

Department of Education and Science (DES) (1988c) *Report of the Committee of Inquiry into the Teaching of English Language.* Chairman Sir John Kingman. London, HMSO.

Department of Education and Science (DES) (1988d) *National Curriculum Task Group on Assessment and Testing. A Report.* London, DES.

Department of Education and Science (DES) (1988e) *Report by Her Majesty's Inspectors on a Survey of Personal and Social Education Courses in Some Secondary Schools.* London, DES.

Department of Education and Science (DES) (1989a) *Initial Teacher Training: Approval of Courses* (Circular 24/89). London, DES.

Department of Education and Science (DES) (1989b) *Education Reform Act 1988: Temporary Exceptions from the National Curriculum.* London, DES.

Department of Education and Science (DES) (1989c) *National Curriculum: From Policy to Practice.* London, DES.

Department of Education and Science and Her Majesty's Inspectors of Schools (DES, HMI) (1977) *Curriculum 11–16.* London, DES.

Desforges, C. (1989) *Testing and Assessment.* London, Cassell.

Dessent, T. (1987) *Making the Ordinary School Special.* Lewes, Falmer Press.

Diener, C.I. and Dweck, C. (1978) An analysis of learned helplessness: continuous changes in performance, strategy, and achievement cognitions following failure. *Journal of Personality and Social Psychology*, 36, 451–62.

Donaldson, M. (1978) *Children's Minds.* London, Fontana.

Doyle, W. (1983) Academic work. *Review of Educational Research*, 53, 159–99.

Doyle, W. (1986) Classroom organisation and management. In M.C. Wittrock (ed.) *Handbook of Research on Teaching* (3rd edn). New York, Macmillan.

Doyle, W. and Carter, K. (1984) Academic tasks in classrooms. *Curriculum Inquiry*, 14, 129–49.

Driver, R. (1983) *The Pupil as Scientist.* Milton Keynes, Open University Press.

Dugdale, R.L. (1977) *The Jukes: A Study on Crime, Pauperism, Disease and Heredity* (5th edn). New York, G. T. Putnam.

Duncan, A. and Dunn, W. (1988) *What Primary Teachers Should Know About Assessment.* London, Hodder and Stoughton.

Dunham, J. (1984) *Stress in Teaching.* London, Croom Helm.

Dürkheim, E. (1952) *Suicide.* London, Routledge and Kegan Paul.

Dweck, C., Davidson, W., Nelson, S. and Enna, B. (1978) Sex differences in learned helplessness: the contingencies of evaluative feedback in the classroom and an experimental analysis. *Developmental Psychology*, 14, 268–76.

Dweck, C. and Wortman, C. B. (1982) Learned helplessness, anxiety and achievement motivation. In H.W. Krohne and L. Laux (eds) *Achievement, Stress and Anxiety*. London, Hemisphere.

Edelwick, J. and Brodsky, A. (1980) *Burn-out: Stages of Disillusionment in the Helping Professions*. New York, Human Sciences Press.

Edwards, A. (1984) *The Development of Self in the Pre-school Child*. Unpublished PhD Thesis, University of Wales.

Edwards, A. (1988) A child of four could tell you. In F. Fransella and L. Thomas (eds) *Experimenting With Personal Construct Psychology*. London, Routledge and Kegan Paul.

Eisner, E.W. (1985) *The Educational Imagination: On the Design and Evaluation of School Programs*. London, Macmillan.

Evans, R. and Ferguson, N. (1974) Screening school entrants. *Association of Educational Psychologists Journal*, 3, 2–9.

Fisher, C.W., Filby, N.N., Marliave, R., Cahe, L.S., Dishaw, M.M., Moore, J.E. and Berliner, D.C. (1978) *Teaching Behaviours, Academic Learning Time and Student Achievement*. San Francisco, BTES: Far West Laboratory.

Floyd, A. (1981) *Developing Mathematical Thinking*. London, Addison Wesley for the Open University Press.

Fogelman, K. (1976) *Britain's Sixteen Year Olds*. London, National Children's Bureau.

Fontana, D. (1984) Failures of academic achievement. In A. Gale and A.J. Chapman (eds) *Psychology and Social Problems*. London, Macmillan/BPS.

French, J. and French, P. (1984) Gender imbalances in the primary classroom: an interactionist account. *Educational Research*, 26, 127–36.

French, J.P. and Peskett, R. (1986) Control instructions in the infant classroom. *Educational Research*, 28, 210–19.

Galloway, D. (1983) Disruptive pupils and effective pastoral care. *School Organisation*, 3, 245–54.

Galloway, D. (1985a) *Schools and Persistent Absentees*. Oxford, Pergamon.

Galloway, D. (1985b) Update: the school's influence on its pupils' development. *Newsletter of Association for Child Psychology and Psychiatry*, 8, iv, 4–9.

Galloway, D. (1987) Teachers, parents and other professionals. In K. David and T. Charlton (eds) *The Caring Role of the Primary School*. London, Macmillan.

Galloway D. (1990a) *Pupil Welfare and Counselling: An Approach to Personal and Social Edication across the Curriculum*. London, Longman.

Galloway, D. (1990b) *Support for Learning in Tower Hamlets.* Report of the Consultant in Special Educational Needs to the Chief Education Officer. Lancaster, Lancaster University.

Galloway, D. (1990c) Was the GERBIL a Marxist mole? In P. Evans and V. Varma (eds) *Special Education, Past, Present and Future.* London, Falmer Press.

Galloway, D., Ball, T., Blomfield, D. and Seyd, R. (1982) *Schools and Disruptive Pupils.* London, Longman.

Galloway, D., Boswell, K., Panckhurst, F., Boswell, C. and Green, K. (1985) Sources of satisfaction and dissatisfaction for New Zealand primary school teachers. *Educational Research,* 27, 44–51.

Galloway, D. and Goodwin, C. (1987) *The Education of Disturbing Children: Pupils with Learning and Adjustment Difficulties.* London, Longman.

Galloway, D., Panckhurst, F., Buswell, K., Boswell, C. and Green, K. (1986) Sources of stress for primary school head teachers in New Zealand. *British Educational Research Journal,* 12, 281–8.

Galton, M., Simon, B. and Croll, P. (1980) *Inside the Primary Classroom.* London, Routledge and Kegan Paul.

Galton, M. and Simon, B. (eds) (1980) *Progress and Performance in the Primary Classroom.* London, Routledge and Kegan Paul.

Galton, M. and Willcocks, J. (eds) (1983) *Moving from the Primary Classroom.* London, Routledge and Kegan Paul.

Gipps, C., Cross, H. and Goldstein, H. (1987) *Warnock's Eighteen Per Cent: Children with Special Needs in Primary Schools.* Lewes, Falmer Press.

Goacher, B., Evans, J., Welton, J. and Wedell, K. (1988) *Policy and Provision for Special Educational Needs: Implementing the 1981 Education Act.* London, Cassell.

Goldstein, H. (1987) *Multilevel Models in Educational and Social Research.* New York, Oxford University Press.

Goldstein, H. (1988) Comparing schools, In H. Torrance (ed.) *National Assessment and Testing: A Research Response.* Kendal, British Educational Research Association.

Gregory, R.P. (1984) Streaming, setting and mixed ability grouping in primary and secondary schools: some research findings. *Educational Studies,* 10, 209–26.

Griffin, T. (ed.) (1991) *Social Trends,* 21. London, HMSO.

Habermas, J. (1972) *Knowledge and Human Interests.* London, Heinemann.

Hamblin, D. (1978) *The Teacher and Pastoral Care.* Oxford, Blackwell.

Hargreaves, A. (1986) Ideological recordbreakers. In P. Broadfoot (ed.) *Profiles and Records of Achievement.* Eastbourne, Holt Educational.

Hargreaves, A. (1988) *Personal and Social Education: Choices and Challenges.* Oxford, Blackwell.

Hargreaves, D. (1967) *Social Relationships in a Secondary School.* London, Routledge and Kegan Paul.

Hargreaves, D. (1982) *Challenge for the Comprehensive School: Culture, Curriculum, Community.* London, Routledge and Kegan Paul.

Harlen, W. (1989) The National Curriculum in science. In *Primary Education and the National Curriculum.* Association for the Study of Primary Education.

Harlen, W., Darwin, A., and Murphy, M.C. (1977) *Match and Mismatch: Raising Questions.* Edinburgh, Oliver and Boyd.

Harré, R. (1979) *Social Being.* Oxford, Blackwell.

Harré, R. (1983) *Personal Being.* Oxford, Blackwell.

Harrop, A. (1983) *Behaviour Modification in the Classroom.* London, Hodder and Stoughton.

Haviland, D. (1988) *Take Care, Mr. Baker!*, London, Fourth Estate.

Heal, K.H. (1978) Misbehaviour among school children: the role of the school in strategies for prevention. *Policy and Politics,* 6, 321–32.

Hearnshaw, L.S. (1979) *Cyril Burt: Psychologist.* London, Hodder and Stoughton.

Hegarty, S. (1987) *Meeting Special Needs in Ordinary Schools.* London, Cassell.

Hewison, J. and Tizard, J. (1980) Parental involvement and reading attainment. *British Journal of Education Psychology,* 50, 209–15.

Hindley, C.B. and Owen, C.F. (1978) The extent of individual changes in IQ for ages between 6 months and 17 years in a British longitudinal sample. *Journal of Child Psychology and Psychiatry,* 19, 329–50.

Hockaday, F. (1984) Collaborative learning with young children. *Educational Studies,* 10, 237–42.

Holdaway, E.A. (1978) Facet and overall satisfaction of teachers. *Education Administration Quarterly,* 14, 30–47.

Holt, M. (1987) Bureaucratic benefits. *Times Educational Supplement,* 18 September, 30.

Honess, T., Murphy, C. and Tann, R. (1983) Reading problems and the child's identity: a construct theory analysis of infant schoolboys and male adolescents. *Human Learning,* 2, 187–208.

Horton, T. and Raggatt, P. (eds) (1982) *Challenge and Change in the Curriculum.* London, Hodder and Stoughton.

House of Commons (1987) Education, science and arts committee, *3: Report: Special Educational Needs: Implementation of the 1987 Act,* HMSO.

Humphries, S. (1981) *Hooligans or Rebels? An Oral History of Working Class Childhood and Youth, 1889–1939.* Oxford, Blackwell.

Inner London Education Authority (ILEA) (1985) *Equal Opportunities for All?* (The Fish Report). London, ILEA.

Inner London Education Authority (ILEA) (1988) *The Primary Language Record: Handbook for Teachers*. London, Centre for Language in Primary Education, ILEA.

Johnson, D.W. and Johnson, R. (1982) *Joining Together Group Theory and Group Skills*. Englewood Cliffs, NJ, Prentice-Hall.

Johnson, D. and Ransom, E. (1983) *Family and School*. London, Croom Helm.

Joseph, K. (1983) *Address to Council of Local Education Authorities*. 16 July. Unpublished.

Kamin, L.J. (1974) *The Science and Politics of IQ*. New York, Erlbaum.

Kelly, A.V., Kimbell, R.A., Patterson, V.J., Saxton, J. and Stables, K. (1987) *Design and technological activity: a framework for assessment*. London, HMSO.

Kelly, G. (1955) *A Theory of Personality*. New York, Norton.

Knight, P. and Smith, L. (1989) In search of good practice. *Journal of Curriculum Practice*, 21, 427–40.

Kohlberg, L. (1975) The cognitive developmental approach to moral education. *Phi Delta Kappa*, 56, 670–7.

Kolvin, I., Garside, R.D., Nicol, A.R., Macmillan, A., Wolstenholme, F. and Leitsch, I.M. (1981) *Help Starts Here: The Maladjusted Child in the Ordinary School*. London, Tavistock.

Lang, P. (ed.) (1988) *Thinking About Personal and Social Education in the Primary School*. Oxford, Blackwell.

Law, B. (1984) *Uses and Abuses of Profiling*. London, Harper and Row.

Levitt, E. E. (1963) Results of psychotherapy with children: a further evaluation. *Behaviour, Research and Therapy*, 1, 45–51.

Light, P., Sheldon, S. and Woodhead, M. (eds) (1991) *Learning to Think*. London, Routledge.

Lynas, W. (1985) *Integrating the Handicapped into Ordinary Schools: A Study of Hearing Impaired Pupils*. London, Croom Helm.

McClure, S. (1989) *Education Reformed*. London, Hodder and Stoughton.

McNamara, D. (1988) Objectives or aspirations? *Review* (of the Education Section of the British Psychological Society), 12, ii, 39–47.

Macbeth, A (1984) *The Child Between: A Report on School–Family Relations in Countries of the EEC*. European Community, HMSO.

Marland, M. (1985) Parents, schooling and the welfare of pupils. In P. Ribbins (ed.) *Schooling and Welfare*. Lewes, Falmer Press.

Maslow, A.H. (1970) *Motivation and Personality* (2nd edn). New York, Harper and Row.

Mead, G.H. (1934) *Mind, Self and Society*. Chicago, Chicago University Press.

Measor, L. and Woods, P. (1984) *Changing Schools Perspectives on*

Transfer to Comprehensive School. Milton Keynes, Open University Press.

Merrett, F. and Wheldall, K. (1986) Observing pupils and teachers in classrooms (OPTIC): a behavioural observation schedule for use in schools. *Educational Psychology*, 6, 57–70.

Merrett, F. and Wheldall, K. (1988) The behavioural approach to teaching with secondary aged children (BATSAC). *Training Package*. Birmingham, Positive Products.

Merrett, F. and Wheldall, K. (1990) Does Batpack training of teachers lead to higher pupil productivity? *Educational and Child Psychology* 7 (i) 31–43.

Metge, J. and Kinloch, P. (1978) *Talking Past Each Other: Problems of Cross Cultural Communication*. Wellington, New Zealand, Victoria, University of Wellington.

Middleton, D. and Edwards, D. (eds) (1990) *Collective Remembering*. London, Sage.

Ministry of Education (ME) (1963) *Half Our Future* (The Newsome Report). London, HMSO.

Mitchell, S. and Rosa, P. (1981) Boyhood behaviour problems as precursors of criminality: a fifteen year follow-up. *Journal of Child Psychology and Psychiatry*, 22, 19–33.

Moon, C. (1984) Making use of miscues when children read aloud. In *Children Reading to Their Teachers*. National Association for the Teaching of English.

Mortimore, J. and Blackstone, T. (1982) *Disadvantage and Education*. London, Heinemann.

Mortimore, P., Sammons, P., Stoll, G., Lewis, D. and Ecob, R. (1988) *School Matters: The Junior Years*. Wells, Open Books.

Moyle, D. (1979) Informal testing and reading needs. In M. Raggett, C. Tutt, and P. Raggett (eds) *Assessment and Testing of Reading: Problems and Practices*. London, Ward Lock Educational.

Nash, R. (1983) Four charges against TOSCA. *New Zealand Journal of Educational Studies*, 18, 154–65.

National Curriculum Council (NCC) (1989a) *Curriculum Guidance 2: A Curriculum for All: Special Educational Needs in the National Curriculum*. York, NCC.

National Curriculum Council (NCC) (1989b) *Interim Report to the Secretary of State on Cross-Curricular Issues*. York, NCC.

Newson, J. (1974) Towards a theory of infant understanding. *Bulletin of the British Psychological Society*. 27, 251–7.

Newson, J. (1977) An intersubjective approach to the systematic description of mother–infant interaction. In H.R. Schaffer (ed.) *Studies in Mother–Infant Interaction*. London, Academic Press.

Nicholls, J. (1984) *Advances in Motivation and Achievement: Vol. 3. The Development of Achievement Motivation*. London, JAI Press.

Nisbet, J. and Shucksmith, J. (1986) *Learning Strategies*. London, Routledge and Kegan Paul.

Norman, D.A. (1978) Notes towards a complex theory of learning. In A.M. Lesgold, J. W. Pellegrino, S. D. Fokkema and R. Glaser (eds) *Cognitive Psychology and Instruction*. New York, Plenum.

Noss, R., Goldstein, H., and Hoyles, C. (1989) Graded assessment and learning hierarchies in mathematics. *British Educational Research Journal*, 15, 109–20.

Nuttall, D. (1981) *School Self-Evaluation: Accountability with a Human Face*. London, Schools Council.

Nuttall, D. and Goldstein, H. (1986) Profiles and graded texts: the technical issues. In P. Broadfoot (ed.) *Profiles and Records of Achievement*. London, Holt, Rinehart and Winston.

O'Leary, K.D. and O'Leary, S.C. (1979) *Classroom Management: The Successful Use of Behaviour Modification in the Classroom*. New York, Pergamon.

Pearson, L. and Lindsay, G. (1986) *Special Needs in the Primary School*. Windsor, NFER-Nelson.

Pervin, L. (1984) Am I me or am I the situation? In P. Barnes, J. Oates, J. Chapman, V. Lee and P. Czerniewska (eds) *Personality, Development and Learning*. London, Hodder and Stoughton.

Phillips, T. (1985) Beyond Lip-service: discourse development after the age of nine. In G. Wells and J. Nicholls (eds) *Language and Learning: An Interactional Perspective*. Lewes, Falmer Press.

Piaget, J. (1936) *The Origin of Intelligence in the Child* (trans. M. Cook, 1977). Harmondsworth, Penguin.

Piaget, J. (1965) *The Moral Judgement of the Child*. New York, Free Press.

Pollard, A. and Tann, S. (1987) *Reflective Teaching in the Primary School*. London, Cassell.

Powell, J.L. (1985) *Ways of Teaching English*. Edinburgh, SCRE Publication No. 86.

Pratt, J. (1985) The attitudes of teachers. In J. Whyte, R. Deem, L. Kant and M. Cruikshank (eds) *Girl-Friendly Schooling*. London, Methuen.

Preston, R.C. (1962) Reading achievement of German and American children. *School and Society*, 90, 350–4.

Pring, R.A. (1984) *Personal and Social Education in the Curriculum*. London, Hodder and Stoughton.

Pritchard, K. and Richmond, K. (1989) *The Records of Achievement Manual*. New York, Longman.

Pumfrey, P. (1979) Which test? In M. Raggett, C. Tutt and P. Raggett (eds) *Assessment and Testing of Reading: Problems and Practices*. London, Ward Lock Educational.

Purkey, S.C. and Smith, M.S. (1983) Effective schools: a review. *Elementary School Journal*, 83, 427–52.

Rabinowitz, A. (1981) The range of solutions: a critical analysis. In B. Gilham (ed.) *Problem Behaviour in the Secondary School: A Systems Approach*. London, Croom Helm.

Ramasut, A. (ed.) (1989) *Whole School Approaches to Special Needs*. Lewes, Falmer Press.

Reynolds, D. (1976) When pupils and teachers refuse a truce: the secondary school and the creation of delinquency. In G. Mungham and G. Pearson (eds) *Working Class Youth Culture*. London, Routledge amd Kegan Paul.

Reynolds, D. (ed.) (1985) *Studying School Effectiveness*. Lewes, Falmer Press.

Reynolds, D. (1991) School effectiveness and school improvement in the 1990s. *Newsletter of Association for Child Psychology*, 13, ii, 5–9.

Reynolds, D. and Murgatroyd, S. (1977) The sociology of schooling and the absent pupil: the school as a factor in the generation of truancy. In H.C.M. Carroll (ed.) *Absenteeism in South Wales: Studies of Pupils, their Homes and their Secondary Schools*. Swansea, Faculty of Education, University College of Swansea.

Richards, M. and Light, P. (eds) (1986) *Children of Social Worlds*. Cambridge, Polity Press.

Roberts, T. (1979) The hidden curriculum in the infants school. *Durham and Newcastle Research Review*, 8, 42, 29–33.

Rubinstein, D. (1969) *School Attendance in London, 1870–1904: A Social History*. Hull, University of Hull.

Rutter, M. (1966) *Children of Sick Parents: An Environmental and Psychiatric Study*. Institute of Psychiatric Study. Institute of Psychiatry, Mandsley Monographs No 16. London, Oxford University Press.

Rutter, M. (1981) Stress, coping and development: some issues and some questions. *Journal of Child Psychology and Psychiatry*, 22, 323–56.

Rutter, M., Cox, A., Tupling, C., Berger, M. and Yule, W. (1975) Attainment and adjustment in two geographical areas: 1. The prevalence of psychiatric disorder. *British Journal of Psychiatry*, 126, 493–509.

Rutter, M. and Madge, N. (1976) *Cycles of Disadvantage*. London, Heinemann.

Rutter, M., Maughan, B., Mortimore, P. and Ouston, T. (1979) *Fifteen Thousand Hours: Secondary Schools and their Effects on Pupils*. London, Open Books.

Rutter, M., Tizard, J. and Whitmore, K. (1970) *Education, Health and Behaviour*. London, Longman.

Ryder, J. and Campbell, L. (1988) *Balancing Acts in Personal, Social and Health Education*. London, Routledge.

Safer, D.J. (1987) *School Programmes for Disruptive Adolescents*. Baltimore, University Park Press.

Salmon, P. and Claire, H. (1984) *Classroom Collaboration*. London, Routledge and Kegan Paul.

Sampson, O.C. (1975) *Remedial Education*. London, Routledge and Kegan Paul.

Schaffer, H.R. (1977) *Mothering*. London, Fontana.

Scottish Education Department (SED) (1978) *The Education of Pupils with Learning Difficulties in Primary and Secondary Schools: A Progress Report by Her Majesty's Inspectorate*. Edinburgh, HMSO.

Secondary Science Curriculum Review (SSCR) (1983) *Science Education 11–16: Proposals for Action and Consultation*. London, SSCR.

Sharp, R. and Green, A.G. (1975) *Education and Social Control*. London, Routledge and Kegan Paul.

Shayer, M. and Adey, P. (1981) *Towards a Science of Science Teaching*. London, Heinemann.

Shipman, M. (1983) *Assessment in Primary and Middle Schools*. London, Croom Helm.

Shotter, J. (1984) *Social Accountability and Selfhood*. Oxford, Blackwell.

Simmons, K. (1986) Painful Extractions. *Times Educational Supplement*, 17 October.

Simon, B.(1989) *The Great Schooling Scandal*. London, Lawrence and Wishart.

Simons, H. (1987) *Getting to Know Schools in a Democracy*. Lewes, Falmer Press.

Skilbeck, M. (ed.) (1984) *Evaluating the Curriculum in the Eighties*. London, Hodder and Stoughton.

Smith, D.J. and Tomlinson, S. (1989) *The School Effect: A study of multi-racial comprehensives*. London, Policy Studies Institute.

Stenhouse, L. (1975) *An Introduction to Curriculum Research and Development*. London, Heinemann Educational.

Stone, M. (1981) *The Education of the Black Child in Britain*. London, Fontana.

Sutherland, M. (1988) *Theory of Education*. London, Longman.

Sutton, A. (1983) An introduction to Soviet developmental psychology. In S. Meadows (ed.) *Developing Thinking*. London, Methuen.

Swann, W. (1985) Is the integration of children with special needs happening? An analysis of recent statistics for pupils in special schools. *Oxford Review of Education*, 11, 3–18.

Swann, W. (1991) *Segregation Statistics: English LEAs. Variations between LEAs in levels of Segregation in Special Schools 1982–1990*. London, Centre for Studies in Integration in Education.

Tajfel, H. (1978) Intergroup behaviour: II Group perspectives. In H. Tajfel and C. Fraser (eds) *Introducing Social Psychology*. London, Penguin.

Tann, C.S. (1981) Grouping and group work. In B. Simon and J. Willcocks (eds) *Research and Practice in the Primary Classroom.* London, Routledge and Kegan Paul.

Taylor, C. (1977) What is human agency? In T. Mischel (ed.) *The Self: Psychological and Philosophical Issues.* Oxford, Blackwell.

Thomas, G. (1982) *The Experience of Handicap.* London, Methuen.

Tizard, B., Blatchford, P., Berke, J., Farquhar, C. and Plewis, I. (1988) *Young Children at School in the Inner City.* Hove, Erlbaum.

Tizard, B. and Hughes, M. (1984) *Young Children Learning.* London, Fontana.

Tizard, J., Schofield, W.N. and Hewison, J. (1982) Collaboration between teachers and parents in assisting children's reading. *British Journal of Educational Psychology,* 52, 1–15.

Tobin, D. and Pumfrey, P. (1976) Some long-term effects of the remedial teaching of reading. *Educational Review,* 29, 1–12.

Tomlinson, S. (1980) The educational performance of ethnic minority children. *New Community,* 8, 213–234.

Tomlinson, S. (1982) *The Sociology of Special Education.* London, Routledge and Kegan Paul.

Tomlinson, S. (1984) *Home and School in Multicultural Britain.* London, Batsford.

Torrance, H. (ed.) (1988) *National Assessment and Testing: A Research Response.* British Educational Research Association.

Training Agency (1990) *Youth Cohort Study: Education and Training Opportunities in the Inner City.* Bradford, Training Agency.

Trayers, M. (1989) The TVEI flexible learning development and extension. In *TVEI Developments: 10, Flexible Learnings.* Sheffield, Training Agency.

Trevarthen, C. (1974) Conversations with a one month old. *New Scientist,* 62, 230–35.

Trevarthen, C. (1977) Descriptive analyses of infant communicative behaviour. In H.R. Schaffer (ed.) *Studies in Mother–Infant Interaction.* London, Academic Press.

Trevarthen, C. (1979) Instincts for human understanding and for cultural cooperation: their development in infancy. In M. Von Cranach, K. Foppa, W. Le Peines and D. Ploog (eds) *Human Ethology.* Cambridge, Cambridge University Press.

Tutt, N. (1985) The unintended consequences of integration. *Educational and Child Psychology,* 2, iii, 30–8.

Tyler, S. (1980) *Keele Pre-school Assessment Guide.* Windsor, NFER-Nelson.

Vincent, D., Green, L., Francis, J. and Powney, J. (1983) *A Review of Reading Tests.* Windsor, NFER-Nelson.

Vogelaar, L. M. E. and Silverman, M. S. (1984) Non-verbal communication in cross-cultural counselling: a literature view. *International Journal for the Advancement of Counselling,* 7, 41–57.

Vygotsky, L.S. (1962) *Thought and Language.* New York, Wiley.

Vygotsky, L.S. (1978) In M. Cole, V. John-Steiner, S. Scribner and E. Souberman (eds) *Mind in Society.* Cambridge, Mass., Harvard University Press.

Walden, R. and Walkerdine, V. (1985) *Girls and Mathematics: From Primary to Secondary Schooling.* Bedford Way Paper No 24. London, Institute of Education, University of London.

Walkerdine, V. (1984) Developmental psychology and the child-centred pedagogy: the insertion of Piaget in early education. In M.J. Henriques, W. Hollway, C. Urwin, C. Venn and V. Walkerdine (eds) *Changing the Subject.* London, Methuen.

Walkerdine, V. and Sinha, C. (1978) The internal triangle: language, reasoning and the social context. In I. Markova (ed.) *The Social Context of Language.* Chichester, Wiley.

Waterhouse, P. (1988) *Supported Self-Study: An Introduction for Teachers.* NCET.

Watts, M. and Bentley, D. (1987) Constructivism in the classroom: enabling conceptual change by words and deeds. *British Educational Research Journal*, 17, 121–35.

Wedge, P. and Essen, J. (1982) *Children in Adversity.* London, Pan.

Wedge, P. and Prosser, U. (1973) *Born to Fail?* London, Arrow Books.

Weiner, B. (1979) A theory of motivation for some classroom experiences. *Journal of Educational Psychology*, 71, 3–25.

Weiner, B. (1984) Principles for a theory of student motivation and their application within an attributionist framework. In R.E. Ames and C. Ames (eds) *Research on Motivation in Education, Vol I: Student Motivation.* London, Academic Press.

Wells, G. (1981) Becoming a communicator. In G. Wells (ed.) *Learning Through Interaction.* Cambridge, Cambridge University Press.

Wells, G. and Nicholls, J. (1985) (eds) *Language and Learning: an Interactional Perspective.* Lewes, Falmer Press.

Wertsch, J.V. (ed.) (1984) *Culture, Communication and Cognition: Vygotskian Perspectives.* Cambridge, Cambridge University Press.

West, C. and Wheldall, K. (1989) Waiting for teacher: the frequency and duration of times children spend waiting for teacher attention in infant school classrooms. *British Educational Research Journal*, 15, 205–16.

Wheldall, K. (1982) Behavioural pedagogy or behavioural overkill. *Educational Psychology*, 2, 181–4.

Wheldall, K. (1985) The use of behavioural ecology in classroom management. In N. Entwistle (ed.) *New Directions in Educational Psychology.* Vol. 1, *Learning and Teaching.* Lewes, Falmer Press.

Wheldall, K. and Glynn, T. (1989) *Effective Classroom Learning.* Oxford, Blackwell.

Wheldall, K. and Merrett, F. (1984) *Positive Teaching: The Behavioural Approach*. London, Allen and Unwin.

Wheldall, K. and Merrett, F. (1985) The Behavioural Approach to Teaching Package (BATPACK): an experimental evaluation. *British Journal of Educational Psychology*, 55, 65–75.

Wheldall, K., Morris, M., Vaughan, P. and Yin Yuk Ng (1981) Rows v Tables: An example of the use of behavioural ecology in two classes of eleven year-old children. *Educational Psychology*, 1, 171–83.

White, J. (1988) *The Language of Science*. A report prepared for the Assessment of Performance Unit. London, DES.

White, R.W. (1959) Motivation reconsidered: the concept of competence. *Psychological Review*, 66, 297–333.

Whitty, G. and Young, M. (eds) (1976) *Explorations in the Politics of School Knowledge*. Driffield, Nafferton.

Whyte, J. (1983) *Beyond the Wendy House: Sex Role Stereotyping in Primary Schools*. York, Longman.

Widlake, P. and Macleod, F. (1984) *Raising Standards: Parental Involvement Programmes and the Language Performance of Children*. Coventry, Community Education Development Centre.

Willes, M. (1981) Children becoming pupils. In C. Adelman (ed.) *Uttering Muttering*. London, Grant McIntyre.

Willis, P. (1977) *Learning to Labour: How Working Class Kids get Working Class Jobs*. London, Saxon House.

Wood, D, (1988) *How Children Think and Learn*. Oxford, Blackwell.

Woods, P. (ed.) (1980a) *Teacher Strategies*. London, Croom Helm.

Woods, P. (ed.) (1980b) *Pupil Strategies*. London, Croom Helm.

Woods, P. (1984) *Parents and School: A Report for Discussion on Liaison between Parents and Secondary Schools in Wales*. London, Schools Council Publications.

Woods, P. and Hammersley, M. (eds) (1977) *School Experience*. London, Croom Helm.

Woolfolk, A.E. and Nicolich, L.M. (1980) *Educational Psychology for Teachers*. Englewood Cliffs, NJ, Prentice-Hall.

Yeomans, A. (1983) Collaborative group work in primary and secondary schools: Britain and the USA. *Durham and Newcastle Research Review*, 10, 51, 99–105.

Young, P. and Tyre, C. (1983) *Dyslexia or Illiteracy? Realising the Right to Read*. Milton Keynes, Open University Press.

Zeichner, K.M., Tabachnick, B.R. and Densmore, K. (1987) Individual, institutional and cultural influences on the development of teachers' craft knowledge. In J. Calderhead (ed.) *Exploring Teachers' Thinking*. London, Cassell.

Index